To:

G- CODE
AKA
GOD CODE

Demetris Chaven

Thanks! Love!

Enjoy!

Copyright © 2016 Demetrice Chance

Scriptural quotations marked KJV are taken from the King James Version Bible.
Book references come from The Celestine Prophecy by James Redfield

ISBN: 978-0-9975291-0-4

All Rights Reserved. No part of this publication may be reproduced, stored in a retrieval system, or transmitted, in any form or in any means – by electronic, mechanical, photocopying, recording or otherwise – without prior written permission.
Thank you for your support of the author's rights.

Printed in the United States of America.

G- CODE
AKA
GOD CODE
"THE ARENA CHANGES,
BUT THE CODE
STAYS THE SAME"

DEMETRICE
CHANCE

Contents

Acknowledgements vii
Introduction 1
Chapter One: You Are the Code 3
Chapter Two: The G in You 17
Chapter Three: God over Money. 26
Chapter Four: The G Within Your Relationships. 36
Chapter Five: The G in Your Character 49
Chapter Six: Unlocking Women: You Are His World. . 64
Chapter Seven: Unlocking Men: Finding Her in Your Soul. . 80
Chapter Eight: The G within your Race of People 96
Chapter Nine: Unlock the Church within you 111
The Message 119

Acknowledgements

I would like to thank all family and friends. Whether you believed in me through spirit, or truth, or spirit, and truth. The support is well appreciated.

Introduction

PEOPLE WILL NEVER be perfect: that is a fact. Sin will always be a part of the world, but the thing about sin is that it will have you switching from left to right. It destroys the structure in which God created the world to operate on. Sin is nothing more than making something imperfect.

We are all perfect beings because our Creator is perfect. The thing that makes us imperfect is the deception that our unstable emotions create. Emotions and feelings are nothing more than a lie that your mind creates. We all know that emotions change every day, and emotions change us. The feelings we go through life thinking we have don't even really exist, but since we allow them to, they change us. Emotions change our actions, thoughts, perceptions, habits, and, all other ways of making decisions.

God never created us to change; He wants us to be who we are. He wants us to be a better version of ourselves every day. The thing that stops us is our never-changing emotions. Every day we are somebody different, never being consistent as to who we are in God. God doesn't change, so why do we change?

The only way to defeat sin, while still sinning, is to live by God's laws, principles, word, and covenant. Learn to be consistent in living by the same principles every day. Being consistent defeats all emotions, because you have decided to obey the same laws, no matter the circumstances. Whether you are sad, happy, tired, or disappointed, you still choose to follow God's principles.

We are all in different walks of life, doing different things. The thing we have to understand about life is that everything in life relates. The principles you used in one arena will work in all arenas. An arena can be you, your body, a football field, a classroom, the dating scene, business, a barbershop, college, your career, politics, and even the clothes you wear. God's principles work in every part of life. Whether you are up or down, rich or poor, winning or losing, you should stay consistent. You may be sinning, but you are still keeping God's structure intact. The arena may change, but the code stays the same.

CHAPTER ONE

YOU ARE THE CODE

UNLOCK THE CODE inside of you! Deep down inside of you is where God is. That is where most people are scared to go. I dare you to travel that road that's so close but yet so far away, that road that no one can travel but you. It's a lonely road, where you are by yourself, and no one else can fit but you and God. You would feel as if you were in the HOV lane.

You've been doing what the Devil wanted you to do all this time, maybe because living for the Devil is comfortable. For example, you may have gone to college, received a good-paying job, live in a good neighborhood, drive a good car, and are living a good life. Not saying that something is wrong with all these things, but humans in everyday life seem to have a "monkey see, monkey do" mentality. Everyone's definition of success is for the most part the things I recently named, and everyone's definition of success shouldn't be the same, but a lot of times it is. God is not a monkey see, monkey do God.

"Now faith is the substance of things hoped for, the evidence of things not seen"- Hebrews 11:1 KJV (King James Version). Key phrase, "things not seen," meaning real faith comes from what we don't see, or what hasn't been done yet. See, going to college and getting a good job are things that can be seen, because they have been repeated plenty of times. God didn't repeat when he created you, he created the first and last you that there will be.

Going to college and getting a good-paying job are just big examples that are practiced every day. I am not trying to single out any group of people. Millions of people have gone to college and received a good-paying job. Again there is nothing wrong with that, but it is at the point where it has become a norm in society: where a lot of individuals in the world are doing what the next individual has already done. Ask yourself, "What can I do that hasn't been done?" Or if it has been done, "In what way can I do it that hasn't been done?" God will give you your own specific answer. I say the answer is "your way," and "the way God wants you to do it."

Now your time has come and passed like everyone else, so you may think it's too late to figure out what God has for you. You may think God told you to do all the things that the majority of people do in life. You may think God is a comfortable God. You may think God is a copycat. Have you done anything for God? Did you obtain all you obtained because you're living for God or living for yourself?

Do you even know who you are? Yeah, you made it,

but did you *really* make it? Yeah, you've grown by nature, but are you really grown, because grown people take chances. Are you scared at how great you could be? And I am not talking about being rich or famous, just being great in your own skin.

Take a moment to look around you. Look at the people in your life. I'm talking about your mother, father, brother, sister, best friend, aunts, uncles, associates, and friends. Now say good-bye to them. I am for real, "Say good-bye to them!" There's nothing they can do for you. Now look at all your belongings—your phone, car, clothes, money, and everything you cherish—and say good-bye to them, too.

You are on a road with God, and all those things you said good-bye to will come back if they're meant to be. Now you are doing things God's way. You are being stripped of all the lies you had for yourself, thinking that what you were doing was the real you. Yeah, the Devil is going to take everything from you, and God is going to let the Devil do it. Whether you know it or not; God is allowing the Devil to do what he is going to do to you, and that is only leading you to Him (God).

God is very strategic in everything he does. God is going to let the devil take everything from you to see if you are strong enough to keep turning that key to unlock your real true self. Keep walking and don't look back; in just a minute your life is going to cave in on you. *The options you once had will be taken from you.* You are going to become a prisoner to yourself. You are going to be stripped of everything you have and everything you had feelings for or loved. You are to become naked again. You are starting over from ground zero, the bottom. A newborn person in the making.

Don't be scared! God is going to give you back everything you lost. He wants you to do things His way now. His way doesn't consist of money, fame, popularity, comfort, feelings, or any of those things that feel good to your body or make you look good. Your flesh is going to start hating you, but your soul is about to start loving you. You are going to feel like a baby again; the way you see things will be brand-new. Kind of like a new world. You are about to learn a new language, a new trade, and your life is going to reverse itself in front of your eyes.

It's about to get so serious, you're going to ask yourself, "What in the Heaven is going on?" And you won't even be able to open your mouth and tell anybody, because it will be unexplainable. You will be at a loss for words; you won't be able to put together a correct sentence to break down what is going on within you.

The only thing you will be able to say is, "*I just know!*" Because God will make you feel like you know the end result, but not know anything in between. Remember these three words— "*I just know*": they're going to come in hand.

The road is going to be dark, because no one can see what is going on with you. You don't even know what is going on with you; you're just letting God take control.

Was your life really real, were you really who you

thought you were, were those people really on your team like you thought they were? Did you really need those cars, clothes, and money like you thought you did? Was that lifestyle all you really thought it was?

Uncomfortable

You can turn around and get back to being comfortable in your nice sheets that keep you warm, or you can become a person that is warm without sheets. You can become a person that doesn't like to be comfortable. You can fly while you're walking, and you can be rich while you're broke. You can look down and see the whole world. You can be loud while being silent. You can drive with no car. You can move while being still.

It's a seed deep down inside of you that hasn't germinated yet. You see the tree, but you don't see the seed that created the tree. You see the roots, the branches, the width of the tree, the beauty, the shade it gives, the fruits it produces, and the nest that lives on it, but you don't see the code that was unlocked inside the seed that produced that amazing object. You see the butterfly but you don't see the cocoon. You see the butterfly flying, doing what it wants to do, but the cocoon was limited to what it could do.

The reason why you didn't see the cocoon or the seed is because God works in silence; He works in the dark, where no one can see what he is doing. He doesn't want anyone to know the secret He puts inside of you. He makes it so that no one can unlock your code. He doesn't want anyone to see what He is doing. You see the seed, but you don't see what's inside of it until it explodes. Then, even when it explodes, you don't know what made it explode. He created the code, and the code is between Him and the Creation.

Unlike trees, butterflies, and all other animals and plants, we humans have free will to unlock the code inside of us or to keep it locked. Most people keep it locked, because they are scared to face what's inside of them. The code is something you are not able to see, only feel, and most humans only follow what they can see, which is not Godly. *"While we look not at the things which are seen, but at the things which are not seen: for the things which are seen are temporal; but the things which are not seen are eternal"- 2 Corinthians 4:18 KJV.* Are you able to see God? No, but you know he is in you. It is something in all of us that is directing us if we allow it to. Doing what you see everybody else does contradicts the reason God created you.

I repeat, going by what you can only see with physical eyes is not Godly. You follow the world and its way of doing things, which is not authentic. *Real people do what they want to do,* because they know who they are on the inside. They know why God created them. They don't have to look at someone else to find out who they are. They don't have to look at their environment to find themselves. What is around them doesn't define them. They don't have to look at their past. They don't have to look at their mistakes. They don't have to look at their situation.

Scared of the Dark

You shouldn't be a problem that can be figured out; if so, then you weren't following the code from the beginning. No one should know why you are the way you are. You don't ever know who you were, because a person who knows who they are: is not able to be figured out. Tell yourself, "*I am not able to be explained; I'm unexplainable.*" They looked on the inside to find themselves. Better yet, they knew who was on the inside by faith, because no one on this planet can see their inside. We will not know what is inside of us until we unlock the code that God gave us. In fact, some people will go to the grave with the code still locked up inside of them.

It's not about what you can see, it's about what you are not able to see. We think figuring people out is a challenge, and will help us, but in reality we are *our own worst enemy.* The only person we need to figure out is ourselves.

I'm about to dig deep into your soul. When most people say "code," they are referring to a way to unlock something, a list of secrets that have to go in a specific order to be unleashed. The code is always within, whether you're talking about a safe where you store money or a locker at school. Say, for instance, the code to unlock your locker is 6- 40-25, and you have to spin it 4 times to the left, then turn right to go to 6, and then spin it in one full circle to the left past 40 and go to 40, then go around to the right to 25 to unlock it. You had to go in all these different directions to finally unlock your locker.

Well, that is how God is—He will take you through

loops, zigzags, and all types of ways to show you what you are not, to bring out the real you. God knows the weird way He created you, but we are born into a world of sin that takes us away from our supernatural state of mind. It's like we are the lock, and we are looking at ourselves wondering, *why am I not able to bring out what is inside of me?* We all have that question inside of us, and God is the only one who can give us the answer.

The world hides "you" from "you," or the Devil hides "you" from "you"—same thing. You are not able to pick the lock, because you do not know yourself. You do not even know that you are locked. You go through life feeling like something is missing, but never wanting to take the time to figure out what it is.

I know most people with some sense have thought to themselves, *If God is so great, why am I not great?* That is the beginning of their journey to God.

Life is like a treasure hunt. You have to use the clues God gives you to figure out what goes where, and when, and why. I wouldn't say you have to go backward, but you do have to retrace your steps. Somewhere down the line, you lost what God gave you because you were too busy focusing on things of the world. The Devil doesn't want you to know who you really are. Believe it or not, the Devil is everyone saying, "I don't think you should do that." Sometimes you probably shouldn't do certain things, like rob a bank, but that's another story for another day. The Devil uses everyone's opinion against you, from your friends to your mother and father.

Going toward the Devil is like driving south down the freeway. You see everything you're doing, including passing up God, basically leaving him behind. You're passing up all the exits, knowing you should have made a U- turn, but going the wrong way feels good to you.

Let's just say, you come to your senses, and you want to go back north toward God. You will have to pass again everything you've seen and done in your past while you were with the Devil. It's like you're passing up an exit you should've taken, but you didn't. It's like figuring out that you were going the wrong way. That is where all the clues come from. You will start seeing why everything was messed up. You are traveling back toward your soul. You were doing everything the world wanted you to do, not even realizing that you were leaving the God in you behind. You thought it was God telling you to do all those things, but it wasn't. You thought because you had that six-figure bank account, had a lavish lifestyle, or a bachelor's or master's degree, that it was God.

See, those things come from worldly desire for the most part. You probably wouldn't even die for any of that. Living for God does not have anything to do with worldly material. You did all those things so the world could bless you, not because it was in your heart. Would you have gotten that degree if you didn't know what was going to come from it? Did you obtain that degree for a certain amount of money? Did you obtain that degree because that is what the world told you that success was?

When you really love something or have a passion for

it, *you do it for free!* You will exhibit that love, whether you win or lose, make money or make no money at all, and have benefits or have no benefits. Love is priceless; it doesn't have a price tag; it doesn't have a motive as to why it does what it does. Love is naked; it doesn't want anything in return for its labor. No clothes, jewelry, or anything. *It doesn't cost to be naked.*

Just like I was saying, you have to turn four times to the right to get to 6. Well, this is just the first turn. God is slowly but surely leading you to 6, unlocking your soul, your true self, because as you are traveling north, you are seeing all your mistakes. You are seeing what worked, and what didn't work. God is showing why certain answers were wrong.

The second turn going toward 6 is when God shows you your mistakes, and may just allow you to commit those mistakes one last time. Except this time, you are aware that you are doing it, so it makes it easier. He will allow your past to be flaunted in your face. It's like retaking a test that you'd failed. See, as He continues to turn the lock, He is making your eyes brand new by the second. You are realizing what you didn't realize at first. The second turn is just a rewind of what you didn't do or see.

The third turn going toward 6 is looking in the mirror and seeing why who you used to be was not who you really were. Like the teacher going over the test with you and telling you why certain answers were wrong, it is a reality check about who you really were. God is mainly telling you why you are the way you are.

The fourth turn before you get to 6 is Him telling you how you can fix it. It feels like a moment of shame. He's making you stare your old self down before He throws the old you in the trash. It is a process of embarrassment. You have to sit there, and hurt, and face the truth until the mirror breaks and there is no truth left. He is helping you move forward with your life. It is like the teacher telling you that he/she is not even going to count the test against you.

Now you are going to the left toward 40. This is after God has showed you about yourself. After He has showed you everything you have done to lose or, should I say, every answer you chose causing you to fail the test. He has to show you your past and then delete it.

See, He doesn't want you to carry your past failures with you. He is basically telling you to exit the freeway and make a left or a right.

This should be the journey where you feel naked like a baby. Everything you see now is new. You don't see life the way you used to see it. He is showing you new things, but while He is showing you new things, you are crawling. You are crawling spiritually, because it's new to you. This is the journey where you are getting yourself together to meet the new you. You are digging yourself out of that spiritual hole that you placed yourself in.

You are basically starting from the bottom, but to other people it will look as if you just picked up where you left off. During this journey you start wearing new clothes, your ideas are new, your passion/drive is new, but you are still naked. He is going to lead you into your new clothes, shoes, ideas, passion, purpose, and all those things. You start to present yourself differently. You don't react to people the same way you used to. You don't do things the same, or do the same things.

God is making you aware of everything that is going on. Your awareness went from a 60 to a 95. The things you use to laugh at, you no longer laugh at. The things that used to make you happy no longer make you happy. Your self-worth is building up little by little daily.

One of the differences is that most people around you will notice the better you, the more advanced you, but they won't accept it. The reason why they won't accept it is because you don't have the results yet. You still have the results of the old you. Everything inside of you has progressed, but you still look the same, as far as your physical appearance. Blessings have yet to hatch.

This is just the fourth turn going toward the second number. Like I said earlier, you are naked, spiritually, because you are being born again. You are figuring out who you really are. So people see the same clothes, situation, person, and status, but all that will soon disappear and will no longer exist. What they don't know is those clothes, status, car, person, or whatever it is that they can physically see on you is only there to hide what God is doing in you. Do you hear me! God works from the inside out, so you may be dirty, busted, and disgusting-looking on the outside, but the inside is looking like Heaven at its finest.

Your attraction to the things and people you used to

like is dying. You are becoming more and more disgusted with your old self, from the activities to the conversations you used to have. You are vomiting all those things up on the inside, but the outside still looks like the old you. Don't worry, let people think that you are the same person; let them believe what they see. Little do they know, you are a whole new creature.

Now it's time to turn back right to 25, the last turn you have to do before unlocking your true self. God is forming the new you now. You are doing everything over, except this time you are doing it His way. You are driving in the lane He wants you in. You are in a new environment going toward things you have not seen before. You want to do things you have not done before. You are not taking your own footsteps. You are not doing what you want to do. This time around, your emotions do not control you. You are doing everything based on your consciousness.

What you spend your money on, what you invest in, and the things that are important are all different to you. You should only be dependent on God. You have a dollar and a purpose. No one is in your corner anymore; all you have is yourself. You are now starting to see what you are really here for. Money is not important in this lane. Nothing is in your way. You don't have friend problems, relationship problems, or drama in your way. You don't know where you are going, but you are believing in God and are letting Him drive. You ran out of gas a long time ago, but God is keeping the car running, or better yet, He is keeping you going. You are a newborn baby that is learning to walk, and God is your Father. He is your father, mother, friend, and sister, replacing everyone and everything you once had. You once had it all—money, status, a nice car—and even though you may still have those things, in reality they don't exist in the world that you live in with God now. You may be grown to the world, but you are a baby to God.

You have unlocked your true self. You get to see all the wonderful things inside of you. Things that you never knew existed. There is a whole lot of gifts inside of your heart. God is amazed at how you put aside your selfish ways and materialistic things to find your true self. You are about to see your purpose and why you are here. Your true meaning to the world is being exposed. You have a new journey that you are about to take. *"But seek ye first the kingdom of god, and his righteousness; and all these things shall be added to you"- Matthew 6:33 KJV.* You have unlocked the Kingdom of God for your life, and now all things are about to be added. In the locker of your heart God has new clothes, cars, money, friends, family, direction, activities, spouse, and lifestyle, which you will have. Now get your book bag out of your locker and go into God's classroom.

Chapter Two
The G in You

BEFORE YOU CAN stick to the code or anything in life, the code has to stick to you. Some of you may ask, "What do you mean when you say that?" Well, what I'm saying is, you have to know who you are to even have a code or stand for anything. And to know who you are, you have to know God. You are not able to be anything God did not create you to be; you will always lose in the process.

God created trees, bushes, birds, black people, white people, lions, tigers, bears, beauticians, basketball players, quiet people, aggressive people, introverts, extroverts, rappers, preachers, fighters, lovers, short people, tall people, and doctors. We all have different instincts. What are instincts? Instincts are basically the things you do without thinking about twice; doing what comes naturally to you. It is a powerful strength of yours that God specifically blessed you with. Also, it is a great God-given relationship that you have with the universe.

A lion is going to be a lion, whether you like it or not. A lion is going to follow his heart. So should you. *Follow your heart, not opinions.* If you were to see a lion attack an animal that came in its territory, you would probably say that is just a lion being a lion, but if a sheep did it, you would probably say that sheep is acting from emotions. We all know sheep don't attack; they are not aggressive. That is not how God made them. That sheep is not being a sheep; it's being fake to itself. The lion acted on its instincts (who you really are), the sheep acted on emotions, not its spirit.

"What? Know ye not that your body is the temple of the holy ghost which is in you, which ye have of God, and ye are not your own? For ye are bought with a price: therefore glorify God in your body, and in your spirit, which are God's"—1 Corinthians 6:19-20 KJV. It's a difference between acting on emotions and being who you are.

In order to know who you are, you have to know your history. Knowing your history is basically thinking about something you came out of your mother's womb doing. Not something you were taught, educated, forced by your peers or family, or grew to do based on your environment. Something you were doing without any help, acknowledgment, or motivation. The way God naturally created you to be.

A lot of people *think that they are what they are around*; that is the confusion that people may have. You are not a product of your environment. People get *lost in themselves, or lost in the sauce*, as some would say. So instead of looking in their heart, subconsciously (naturally doing something that you don't know you are doing) they are looking to what is around them to define them. Therefore, people are walking around acting from emotions. In reality, they are letting their feelings dictate their decisions, being somebody different every day, and never really finding their true spirit. Then people wonder why they are stereotyped into certain social groups. Everybody is doing what the next person is doing. They have no code to stand by, and if you are not being who you are, the code is not going to stand by you. One day they are a sheep and the next day they are a lion, depending on the situation or circumstance they find themselves in. You have to be one or the other, you not able to be both.

"Be sober, be vigilant; because your adversary the devil, as a roaring lion, walketh about, seeking whom he may devour:"- 1 Peter 5:8 KJV. The Devil's job is turn you into something that you are naturally not. Ask God what was your natural personality before you let the world get the best of you. You have to ask yourself, Who am I when I am alone? What do I believe in? Who am I when I am around my friends, family, and people in general? Do I react the same in different situations? Do I put on a new face around certain people, or am I always the same? Does my personality change when I am around certain people?

"For as he thinketh in his heart, so is he: eat and drink, saith he to thee; but his heart is not with thee"- Proverbs 23:7 KJV. So as a man thinks in his heart, so is he. Now ask yourself, do those comparisons add up? If they add up,

then you can stop reading this book now, since I'm not able to help you, but if they don't add up, then this book is just for you.

Now I am not saying you shouldn't adapt, but adapt and change are two different things. When you change is when you become someone else; you act a different way than your normal unbothered self. Now adapt is more of a mental game, like playing chess. You are using your mind, but you are still being you. When you adapt, you *think like the environment you are in, but you move like yourself.*

When we are around people, we tend to live in their world, do what they do, and act how they act, and then wonder why the world views us a certain type of way. The code is not able to help us if we don't help the code. Basically, what I'm saying is we have to be who we are in order to be respected and looked at like the greatness we have in ourselves. You are the answer to all your questions, you are the truth to all your lies, and you are the reason to all your whys.

War with the Devil

There is a challenge to be that person every day. The Devil is going to challenge you every day to see if you are going to keep being that person or change. If you are a nice, kindhearted person, be a nice kindhearted person every day of your life. Don't let anyone or anything change you. If you are aggressive, nonchalant, talkative, calm, laidback, or whatever it is in your Godlike character, then be that way by any means necessary. The moment you allow your situation, environment, friends, family, job, or anything else to change you, then you will be breaking the code of who you are. It's hard to be who you are in a world full of people who treat people how people treat them. Fitting in will get you nowhere. It is exactly how it sounds, "fitting in," like putting on a shirt that doesn't fit, but since you really like that shirt, you are willing to adjust yourself to *fit* that shirt, instead of making a shirt *fit* you.

Make the world fit you, and don't fit the world. You were made to stand out. *"For what shall it profit a man, if he shall gain the whole world, and lose his own soul? Or what shall a man give in exchange for his soul?"-Mark 8:36-37 KJV.* I understand that you have been hurt, mistreated, abused, unloved, talked about, etc., but that shouldn't stop you from being a nice, caring, mysterious, rough person, or whatever natural godlike attributes you may have. Keep the code of character that God placed in your heart from birth.

People follow "worldly wisdom." What is worldly wisdom? It is saying I'm going to treat people how they treat me; I am going to do what everybody else does; I am going to be like everyone else around me. *"And be not conformed to this world: but be ye transformed by the renewing of your mind, that ye may prove what is that good, and acceptable, and perfect, will of God"—Romans 12:2 KJV.* To God, that is a weak way of thinking, but that is what most people do to fit in, or to feel good about themselves. *"For the wisdom of this world is foolishness with God. For it is written, he taketh the wise in their own craftiness"-1 Corinthians 3:19 KJV.*

I understand we all learn from our mistakes, but reacting to them in a way that is not naturally you only opens the door for something else to happen to you. It's like a revolving cycle that only can stop with you. Following the code for God created you to be is going to hurt just as bad as it did when Jesus got nailed to the cross for us. He did not bend or fold on us, but we fold on Him every day, even when He has already paved the way for us.

You have to take all the nails that people are going to nail to you for keeping it *G* (Godly). Do you want to know why? Cause you are saying *the cycle stops with me!* I'm talking about not responding to people who are talking about you, judging you, saying harsh words to you, using you, being snakes to you, and gossiping about you. You have to take all those nails. And what I mean when I say you have to take all those nails is, you do not respond to it or do the same to them. What they do to you, you do to someone else, and someone else does to another person, and then eventually it leads right back to happening to you.

You want to be gangster in God's eyes, you want to be tough in God's eyes, you want to be solid in God's eyes, you want to be real in God's eyes, then not treating people how they treat you is how you do it, and I mean those sayings in a positive light. How do you think Jesus felt when they were nailing him to the cross? He was praying for them, saying, *"Then said Jesus, father, forgive them; for they know not what they do. And they parted his raiment, and cast lots"- Luke 23:34 KJV.* Jesus knew they did not know any better, and they didn't know how their deed was going to affect them. When people don't know any better, you should ignore them. Jesus was being the bigger person, because He was on a higher level of thinking. You not responding to people just shows the level you are on and that you understand something that they may have yet to comprehend. Remember: *it's not what you respond to, but what you don't respond to* that shows how close you are to God.

People think that the things they do are them, when in reality it is learned behavior, kind of like a survival tactic. They respond the way they do based off what has happened to them in their past, or how they were raised. That response naturally becomes them, so now the real them is behind them, while the Devil is in front of them. The Devil leads their actions, but they think it's normal. They only think it is normal because everyone around them accepts the consequences that come with it. They have made it a way of life. They adapted to the situation, but they also let the situation change them subconsciously. They are acting off emotions, thinking it's natural instinct. Think about it; most people in a certain environment act alike.

Love, confidence, and strength are naturally given, so why do we feel we have to prove ourselves? See, our faith in God has declined. We walk around with our guards up when God is our guard. We walk around preplanning how we are going to respond to something without God leading us. Everything we tend to try to do ourselves is what we should let God do; the battle was never ours to begin with.

Take the time to ask yourself, "Is the way I am acting

really me, or did I let the world change me?" Really think about your answer. Think about how you were before the world started judging you and telling you who you had to be. All the times you felt like making the other person feel how you feel has gone to make everything better. All the times you tried to prove yourself instead of just being quiet, and leaving the situation in God's hand. All the times you felt like you had to go out of your way to prove a point.

Most of the time you don't even realize you are doing those things, because they are instilled in you. The bible says*: "The lord is long-suffering, and of great mercy, forgiving iniquity and transgression, and by no means clearing the guilty, visiting the iniquity of the fathers upon the children unto the third and fourth generation."—Numbers 14:18 KJV.* You are not acting like your normal Godlike self; you are acting like your mother, father, grandfather, etc. Just take a step back and look at everything you do and ask, "God, is this really me?" You are going to have to pause your life while you watch everyone else's keep going. Then you will see that people are a little bit of everything. They have picked up ways from everything, and everybody around them, but they are not truly themselves. They are in a trap, because those are the things and people they see every day. You have picked up all those pieces and created a person God doesn't even know. Remember this: *people act like everyone else but themselves.* They are comfortable being the same as everyone else.

Have you noticed the more you change, the more you

don't get anywhere or accomplish anything? For example, you can get change for a dollar bill, which can be four quarters, twenty nickels, or one hundred pennies. At the end of the day, it's still one dollar. You did all that changing and didn't gain anything. (When I speak about dollars, I am speaking as if dollars were your spirit).

So if you consider yourself a dollar bill, sticking to the code will turn you into two dollars tomorrow, then three dollar bills the next day, and so on. *Don't change, get better. You are who you are for a reason.*

Chapter Three
God over Money

I WAS AT Walgreens one day looking as regular as they come. I had just one dollar in my checking account and a lot of money in my savings account, but I had already told myself that I wasn't taking out any more money from my saving's account. All I wanted to buy was some Halls cough drops and some butter pecan ice cream. I had my food stamp card with me, but the food stamp card only paid for the ice cream, so I had to put the Hall's cough drops back, since one dollar wasn't enough to buy them. In my head, I was thinking that the cashier probably thought I didn't have any money. She could be saying to herself, "This man doesn't even have two dollars."

Now, I could've been fake to myself and taken the money out of my saving's account just to look good in front of her, but I would've broken the code. I'm saying all this to say that sticking to the code doesn't always make you look good, it doesn't get you all the attention, people are not going to be cheering you on, nobody is going to understand you, and you may have to take losses, suffer, and be sick to your stomach, but it will get you the best results with God. He will make sure you get what you need.

You may not have the best house, car, money, fame, status, or anything, but at least you can die with your soul still being attached to you. If you say you are not going to do something, then don't do it; don't worry about the circumstances. Let God decide whether or not you have a big house and a lot of money. *He is the result-maker*.

God created the code to make us stronger spiritually. He will put us in situations that will make us look very low on the outside but feel very high on the inside. Sticking to the code will humble you, because a person who is following the code will have days when they will look weak to everybody. I went a whole year without buying myself clothes, shoes, or anything else. I didn't have anything or look like I did, but I had a rich soul. Yeah, *a rich soul with broke decisions*; think about it.

See, when you stand for something, whether you know it or not, you are richer than a person with a million dollars who doesn't stand for something. Are you going to spend your money on clothes, or save it so you can invest in yourself or other ventures? *"But he that is the greatest among you shall be your servant. And whosoever shall exalt himself shall be abased; and he that shall humble himself shall be exalted"-Matthew 23:11-12 KJV.* The people who just live life, always buying clothes, going on trips, spending money on things with no value, will be the same people with nothing to show for all the fun they have. Those people are serving their body for a temporary feeling. A humble person will serve his soul and let the pleasures of the body be served by God. You have to allow yourself to go all the way down for God to raise you all the way up. You have to go without clothes, partying, haircuts, food, dating, friends, or whatever else. You may have to look dirty for a while and not be able to impress anybody.

It is time to get real ugly on the outside. You are going to have to wear those dirty shoes and those same clothes. You are going to have to go without eating for a while. You may even lose weight—I did. In order to become the highest, you have to be the lowest.

It's Not How Much You Make, But How Much You Spend

Let's say, for instance, you went from making $40,000/yr to $80,000/yr. Those same principles you had while making $40,000/yr, you will have to keep applying them as if you are still making that amount. The reason why so many people don't go beyond themselves is because they want to live the lifestyle of their salary. Which in reality makes them break even. You are living on the same level you were living on when you were making $40,000. You make a little more, now you want to do a little more. That is how people fail. They don't give themselves room to breathe, because the more they make, the more they want to buy. They want to look like their job.

You have to look the opposite of your salary. Trying to match the lifestyle of your salary will only put you on the same level as someone who makes less than you. You didn't make your $80,000 look good. Instead, it only made you look good. So you make $80,000/yr, another person makes $30,000/yr, and another $10,000/yr. In reality, depending on how you choose to spend your money, you are no better off than them.

It is not how much you make, but how much you spend. Buy more of what you need and less of what you want. See, having a Godly spirit with your finances determines how rich you really are and can be in the future. The person who makes $30,000/yr can be internally richer than the person who makes $80,000/yr by what he/she spends and saves. Keep the same car, same apartment, same lifestyle, same clothes. Let your money grow, let it multiply, and your spirit will grow, because you are humbling yourself to not look like your bank account. You are not worried about how the outside looks but how the inside looks. This is just another way that God works in the dark.

When you are living according to how much you make, then you are putting your lifestyle in the light, and that is not Godly. A person shouldn't make $80,000/yr. and let others know they make that amount of money by what they wear, drive, and flaunt. On the other hand, when someone makes $80,000/yr. and looks like they make $25,000, then God is working in the dark, because that person's salary is hidden from the world. He is opening doors for you to invest in people, businesses, mutual funds, your kids' future, and things of that nature. Your money is growing without your acknowledgment. You give God 10; God will give you 100. *God only multiplies what you give him when you have been solid to your lifestyle.*

Don't Let Money Get You Excited

You may ask, "What do you mean when you say 'solid to your lifestyle'"? I mean God can trust you, and bless you when things in life don't get you excited. *"Heaviness in the heart of man maketh stoop: but a good word maketh it glad"- Proverbs 12:25 KJV.* Knowing you are receiving a certain amount of money can have you planning too much ahead of time. You saying, "I am going to buy this, pay that, do this for my kids, get out of debt, go shopping." Your mind is going a hundred miles an hour. You are putting all these commands on yourself that is building your heart up to get let down. Then when it doesn't happen, you get sad and disappointed. It is nothing but God saying, "Slow down, little momma. Slow down, little daddy. I got you in due time."

God doesn't want us to get anxious about anything. If you get excited about $80,000, then God will not bless you with $100,000. Would you give someone two hundred dollars if they didn't even know how to budget one dollar? People who tend to blow money never really have money. God gives them a little something to see how they would respond, and they just spend it all.

Everything in life that God gives us is for us to multiply, from our talents to our money, knowledge, and resources. He expects us to come back with more than what He gave us. *People are priceless*, so no amount of money in this world should move us.

When income tax season comes, people expect to get back a few thousand dollars. They may get a little excited to be getting that amount of money back, but they broke the code, because they became excited. I'm not saying that they will not get that amount of money back, but that is the highest amount of money they will receive. Whatever amount of money gets you excited is where you will get comfortable. You will not exceed that limit. You put a ceiling on your God, because you became excited by, let's say, $4,000. God is priceless!

The reason why people can make two million dollars with ease is because they didn't let making one million get them excited. When your focus stays on God and not on a certain amount, as if you are not worth it all, then you can have it all. As long as you continue to not get excited or anxious, or worry, then you are limitless in your finances. You will be able to multiply any amount of money God gives you.

"And Peter answered him and said, lord, if it be thou, bid me come unto thee on the water. And he said, come. And when Peter was come down out of the ship, he walked on the water, to go to Jesus. But when he saw the wind boisterous, he was afraid; and beginning to sink, he cried, saying, lord, save me"- Matthew 14:28-30 KJV. In the Bible, when

Peter took his eyes off Jesus, he began to drown. That is the same with money. As you continue to keep your eyes on God, then you will continue to multiply, but as soon as you take your eyes off God, your money will drown.

People don't even know how to budget two hundred dollars, and that is why they have been stuck in the same predicament for years. People tend to spend on the level they're on. Which leaves them standing in the same spot. You make $80,000 going toward God, but you give it right back to the devil. You were going to the right, but you turned around and went to the left. Now you are back at the same spot. That's a circle in most people's lives. Pick a direction you want to head in, and go that way. Don't look at what you want to buy or could spend your money on, or how good you can look. Just keep going toward God. All the money, cars, and clothes will be there when you're done multiplying.

Paycheck to Paycheck

For a period in my life, I always just had enough to pay my bills. I didn't understand how that happened to me. I didn't really spend my money on anything but food and things like that. After all my bills were paid, I would try to pay my tithes but end up not having money to pay my tithes. I didn't have money to give to God.

God has a way of making you not have any money when you know you should, when you don't give him 10 percent of your paycheck. Money will just have a way of walking out of your pocket. Bills, debt, and other things will just appear that will eat your pockets up.

I was giving to everything else first before I gave to God. I didn't follow the instructions God gave. I should have paid my tithe first, but I gave to my bills and debt first, because my faith in God was low. *Pay god first then pay everything and everybody later.* What you don't give to God, the world won't give to you. *"But this I say, he which soweth sparingly shall reap also sparingly; and he which soweth bountifully shall reap also bountifully"- 2 Corinthians 9:6 KJV.*

Some people may go through life not really taking paying their tithes seriously and wonder why they only have enough money to get by, and tithes don't have to be to a specific church or anything. It may be anything; just make sure your 10 percent is between you and God. When I let God control my finances, I begin to have money in my pocket. I was still just spending money on food and other needs, but now I involved God in my budget.

You also have to put your needs over your wants. In other words, you have to sacrifice your wants for your needs. You have to buy only what you need. Your wants will have to wait. Do not buy clothes and shoes until you are well organized. You may want to go out for drinks or to eat, but your spirit is way more important than your flesh. It will be hard to do, because your flesh will be highly upset that you are not giving it any attention.

Tell yourself that you are only going to spend a certain amount of dollars a paycheck. Sometimes you will have to go without. You will have to live with embarrassment. As far as God goes, He would rather you be on the safe side than down to your last dollar. In Israel, the tax collectors told the Israelites to put money back, so when the tax collectors came to collect they would have money set aside just in case a hard time arose. You would rather be safe than sorry.

God does not believe in putting anything or anybody before Him. Unfortunately, when you have debt, you are not able to fully commit your finances to Him. Debt should be the first thing you take care of after you pay your tithes. It can be a demon that follows you until you get rid of it, just holding you back from moving forward.

Get the Devil Out of Your Pockets

As long as we have debt, we are in slavery to whomever we owe. You are never free if you owe on something, or owe someone, or are paying a car note or something. It is just like borrowing something from somebody and having to pay them back. They own you until you don't have to pay them back. The item is not fully yours, just temporally yours.

In God's eyes you are putting your debt before him. Someone else has control of your life at the moment. *How can God tell you where to go if you're not even the driver?* God is a jealous God; He doesn't want anybody before Him. Make a promise to yourself that you will get off government assistance and take care of all loans and personal debt. I say, "*Get it out the mud.*" In other words,

He is saying do everything yourself. You got everything you need to do it yourself. *All the money you need is inside of you.* Do not ask the devil for help. Don't ask family, friends, government, banks, or any of them for help. I am not saying any of those people or resources are the Devil, but God wants you to depend directly on him.

Chapter Four
The G Within Your Relationships

HAVE YOU EVER been on a ship, a cruise, a boat, or anything that moves on the water? Ships tend to travel a lot of different places, but they have an alignment of operations within the ship that moves together to make the ship move. There is a collective force that is making the boat go where it needs to go. No one ship can move by itself. You know how you have two paddles, and each paddle has to be going back and forth at the same time at the same pace. No paddle can be faster than the other, or the ship will not go anywhere. The ship will be confused as to what it should do. If the paddles were to continue to be offbeat with each other, eventually the ship is going to stay where it is or not really move at its full potential. One paddle may see something that the other paddle doesn't see. The other paddle may not really want to go anywhere. It may be comfortable where it is. One paddle may be on a time limit and may set a certain goal to reach by a certain time, while the other paddle may not be in a rush or even have a goal to reach. One paddle may be focused more on the future of the ship, while the other paddle is still focused on why the ship is the way it is. One paddle may know that the future of the ship is going to look better at the end than it does now, while the other paddle cares about how it looks now. That paddle is embarrassed to be seen with the other paddle based on the situation at hand. One paddle may know that everything is going to be okay when they get where they're going. The ship is going to get fixed, it is going to get to safety, and the ship will get to everything it needs, while the other paddle is worried about the condition of today. One paddle may be willing to go through hell to reach its destiny, while the other paddle wants everything to go its way. One paddle may have faith that the ship can make it through the coming storm, while the other paddle is scared to even go through the storm. One paddle just likes the journey and adventure of where the ship could possibly end up, while the other paddle wants to know where the ship will end up. That paddle wants all the answers now, because this paddle has no faith. It wants to know that there is sunshine on the other side of the ocean before it even sails away. It wants to see the glory, benefits, rewards, and gifts before they are earned.

One paddle wants to get away from its misery, while the other wants to stay there. They both have arms, but one doesn't want to move. Little does the selfish paddle know, if it doesn't move, then the other paddle, ship, or their paddle, is going nowhere. No one benefits from the situation. How do you think the other paddle feels, the paddle that's been putting in all that work, trying to go places it has never been, trying to see things it has never seen? Taking routes that have never been taken. That paddle wants to elevate into its greatness, but the other paddle is holding it back. That is sickening; the paddle wants to act off faith, while the other is scared to take risks. One paddle refuses to not use its strength to knock the waves out of its way, while the other is too scared to even try for the better of the ship. That paddle knows it is better than all the ships around them. That paddle doesn't want to fit in or waste its talent being stagnant sitting in one spot. That paddle is not comfortable being where it is. All along the other paddle is comparing itself to its surroundings. That paddle sees every other paddle, or ship, sitting still, so that's what it does. No other ship went anywhere, so that paddle doesn't want to go anywhere. That paddle thinks it belongs there at the dock with all the other paddles doing nothing but getting rusty. So at the end of the day, the paddle that is comfortable, and the paddle that is not comfortable end up at the same spot.

When you and someone don't see things on the same level, then you all will get nowhere. Both of you are holding each other back. *"Be ye not unequally yoked together with unbelievers: for what fellowship hath righteousness with unrighteousness? And what communion hath light with darkness?"- 2 Corinthians 6:14 KJV.*

Relate

In order to build a relationship with anybody, you have to relate to them first before you can go forward. Relate means you can be connected by blood, family, environment, circumstances, social status, certain habits, or anything else that puts you in a specific mindset, a mindset that allows you to see something in a particular way. Before you create your relationship with this person, ask yourself, "Does this person think like me? Has this person been through what I've been through? Does that person come from the same background or economic status? Does the person have the same understanding about certain situations? How is the environment in which he/she comes from? Do they handle things in the same way? Do all your cultural elements compare with one another's? Are all your ancestors the same? Do you all come from the same bloodline? Are you all connected to the same family tree?

Now I am going to start at the beginning of that verse I mentioned a few lines before, saying "Be ye not unequally yoked together with unbelievers…" and work my way through it in due time. A yoke is a wooden bar that joins two oxen to each other and the burden they pull. Now let me get into depth in the definition of yoke. I notice it said two oxen, not one ox and one lion, not one ox plus one bull, not one oxen plus one tiger. It specifically said two oxen, meaning before you can start traveling, crank up the car, drive, or do anything, the two forces have to be the same. God is specific in what He does. He is not going to have two different animals to pull the same weight, two different cars to use the same motor, or two different kinds of people to drive in the same lane. See those oxen come from the same background, carry the same struggles, have the same bloodline, have the same culture, and see things the same way. Now let's transfer that example into a human aspect. Just like God created different kinds of animals, such as oxen, lions, frogs, tigers, and elephants, He also created different kinds of people, which we call race, such as Negroes, Europeans, Mexicans, Asians, and other kind of people. *"I said in mine heart concerning the estate of the sons of men, that God might manifest them, and that they might see that they themselves are beasts."—Ecclesiastes 3:18 KJV.* Beast referring to animals. Just like different animals of a specific kind live in the same environment, do the same daily routines, build with each other, and pull the weight of each other, we too should do the same, starting with the race we are a part of.

According to God, we should not be yoked to different kind of races or spirits. We as race all pull different weight and have a different task from God. We all have different cultural beliefs and things that we do as a group. Just as He requires the lion to be the king of the jungle and the giraffe to eat leaves off a tree. Only their kind would be able to contribute to their life. Only eagles can help eagles, and only giraffes can help giraffes. Mixing will only throw things off track and have them operating outside their natural nature.

"Ye shall keep my statutes. Thou shall not let thy cattle

gender with a diverse kind: thou shalt not sow thy field with mingled seed: neither shall a garment mingled of linen and woolen come upon thee"- Leviticus 19:19 KJV. Everyone and everything that God created should stay with its own kind. God does not want you to leave the tree from which your roots came. Not one single leaf falls off that tree if God is concerned. Stay on the tree that God placed you on. Keep that spiritual connection intact, because without it you will get nowhere. Where there is no God, there is no destination. Remember, you are trying to get to the point of having a relationship, and ships go places. We too have different requirements based on our race. So before you can become unequally yoked, you have to be with your kind of people. One Negro and European is not valid; the motor won't even start, as far as God is concerned. See when two different kinds of animals and two different kinds of humans can both be going forward in two different directions. Be with your own kind, just as the two oxen.

Relations

After you find out who you are supposed to relate to in God's eyes, then you start having relations with that person. The second part of 2 Corinthians 6:14 says: "Be not unequally yoked together with unbelievers: for what fellowship hath righteousness with unrighteousness?" You have to now figure out whether the both of you are going in the same direction. Having righteousness with unrighteousness is like 2 plus (-2): you only get 0 out of the situation. Now what is the definition of righteousness? Righteousness means being morally upright to God's laws. To break it down a little more, having morals means having principles or rules of right conduct, knowing the difference between right and wrong. To have principles in place means you don't act on emotions, you don't live based on what you see or what makes you feel good. Feelings change every day, but principles don't. Also, you don't allow material things to excite you or carry weight in your life. What people possess shouldn't define the relations you have with them or the direction the two of you are headed in together. Their upright character should determine the relations you have with them. When people think of being equally yoked with someone, they tend to have a worldly view. They think being equally yoked means you and that person are making the same amount of money, living in the same neighborhood, driving the same car, living the same lifestyle, or any other worldly figure that makes you feel like the both of you are equally yoked. Those worldly things don't make you all equal. What is money without character? Don't let a lifestyle buy the relations you have with people. You can both drive the fastest car in the world and still be going nowhere. Being equally yoked in God's eyes means living right according to His principles. The both of you don't judge others or bring each other down, and you all motivate each other with your actions and words. You both have a comparable vision of life. You all do not have a ceiling above you all that makes you all comfortable. You both believe that you want to go as far as God takes you spiritually, mentally, and physically. You both have the mindset to become better each day God gives you, and you never want to get comfortable being the person you were the day before.

You should want to have a relation like the two oxen that were working together in order to go forward. Ask yourself, "How are your relations with people?" You know how you have to put the right gas in your car for it to run properly. The same way you have to put the right tires on your car, or the right motor in your car, for it to go anywhere. It takes a team effort to have a car start effectively. You don't want to be at a green light with all the cars passing you by because you put the wrong motor oil in your car. It is the same way with your life. You have to watch what you allow to get inside of you. It is only certain motor oil that your car can run on. Just like your body can only handle the heart of certain people. You don't want to allow your heart to get involved with the wrong motor, and your heart won't start. Look into people's intentions as to why they are even having relations with you in the first place. Their intentions come from the heart, and if their intentions and your heart aren't on the same page, then your car won't start. They had other things planned, and you thought that they were in it for the long haul. You had an upright heart, but they had unholy intentions. Do the people you associate with have vision? Can they see as far as you? You have to have 20/20 vision in both of your eyes. Are you parallel to each other?

Also, sometimes you may just need a new motor. You

are having unsuccessful relations with people because your heart is not right. You are jealous of your friends, bitter from previous relationships, which keeps you from moving forward, you have resentment in your heart, and all other types of stoppage that keeps your body from cranking up. Your body is your car. Anybody that motivates you to move forward you just push them away. Like a motor just throwing up everything that does it some good. The motor has been mistreated and abused for so long, when good comes along, it doesn't accept it. You can have the best person in your corner, fresh and pure, but your body reneges them because of old abuse. A car that operates on a dead motor cannot move forward, no matter how bad it wants to. As long as you have the same pain, hurt, confusion, lies, and betrayal from other people in your heart, it will stop you from moving forward. But since you are not man-made, all you have to do is clean out your heart, whereas in the case of a motor, you have to buy a whole new one. Take some time to be by yourself. Put yourself in God's Car Shop. Let him work on you for as much time as He needs. Throw up all the bad and allow the good to come in. Take out all the darkness blocking you from seeing the light. Who can travel in the darkness with someone else? You don't want anyone holding you back, and you don't want to hold anyone back.

You have gone through the process of finding who you are supposed to relate to, to having relations with that person, to then forming a relationship all in a way that God intends it to happen. The ship is two people becoming one to move forward. 2 Corinthians 6:14 ends by saying, "Be not unequally yoked together with unbelievers: for what fellowship hath righteousness with unrighteousness? And what communion hath light with darkness?" You are now being connected as one.

Relationship: Positive Force & Negative Force

Now you know when two things are connected as one, there has to be an up and down, a left and right, right and wrong, good and bad, positive and negative, forward and backward, male and female. One has to complement the other. My bad has to be your good, and your good has to be my bad, sort of like a helpmate that God made especially for you. You know how a remote, or anything that needs batteries, has to have a positive and negative energy to operate. That is how life works. Nothing works when it is exactly the same. The batteries see life in the same light, but they are both different at the end of the day. God doesn't want you to have something that is exactly the same as you; that doesn't mean one of you brings each other down, or one is unrighteous and the other isn't, but it means God does not want to complement your strengths but your weaknesses. To God, it does no justice for Him to put you in a relationship with someone just like you. It is like He is just adding to your strengths but ignoring your weaknesses. That will not help you. How can you exercise on an already fit upper body but ignore your lower body? There is no challenge in getting help in an area where you don't need help. God wants you to be the best you can be, so He places you with people that will expose you to your weaknesses to help you. For example, I may like to talk too much and don't feel a need to fix it.

The way God handles your bad habit is to place someone in your life that is the exact opposite. Again, you all may see the same light, take risk, and be righteous, but are still different. So in that case He will place someone in your life that doesn't talk as much. That person will make you confront a part of your life that you have been running from. We are always saying, "He is not my type", "She is not my type", or "I don't have friends or hang around people like that". That type of thinking will leave you on a ship going nowhere. Little do you know that person has a weakness that you can help and that you all will benefit from each other. See, we don't want someone that challenges our weaknesses, but God does. In order for us to move forward, we have to confront our weaknesses. When we run from a challenge or anything that would make us better, we are running from God. We want something that makes us comfortable, because whether we admit or not, we are just like the exact person that makes us comfortable. God doesn't care about what you like, your comfort, your type, or what you want to be around; He cares about what's in your best interest. We often don't see that, and when we do see it, we ignore it because, subconsciously, we are afraid to be better. We all have those types of people and things we like to be around, because it's makes us feel that the way we are is an okay way to be. If it's attractive, turns us on, or fits in with us then we are all for it. That is where we lose. This may sound crazy, but two positives will get you nowhere. Just the same as two negatives. When you are walking, one foot is in front, and the other is in the back. They continuously switch roles. Love God enough to deal with people that can help you, even if they're not your type. For example, You put ice in water to make it cold, and water in the freezer to make it ice. Relationships are here to benefit you in areas you know you need help in. What you don't see about yourself another person can.

Keep-Up

In basketball they have a play called a give-and-go, where one player sets a pick on the defensive player (blocks the defensive player from being able to guard his teammate, who has the ball). He then backs off the pick to get open, and his teammate passes him the ball to score. In order for the play to work to score, both players have to be on one accord. That is how a relationship works. The two of you must put in the same effort and be on the same level for the ship to move. One body should pick up where the other body stops. What I am saying is keep up with your teammate. When they are putting in work or moving forward, you should pick up where they left off and move forward, one leg after the other. The time limit you have for yourself has to be in comparison to your teammate. You don't want them to pass you the ball when you're not ready. You have to be prepared to move, depending on their speed. The faster they move, the faster you have to move. You should not slow them down nor let them slow you down. The more you all are walking with each other, the more challenging it should be for the both of you. *If the relationship doesn't challenge you, then it will go nowhere.* If they are working every day, becoming a better person, pursuing their dream, then so should you, because the ship will go nowhere if one person is leaving the other behind, or the other is not keeping up.

Chapter Five
THE G IN YOUR CHARACTER

"*AND HE SAID, hearken ye, all Judah, and ye inhabitants of Jerusalem, and thou king of Jehoshaphat, thus saith the lord unto you, be not afraid nor dismayed by reason of this great multitude; for the battle is not yours, but God's*" -2 Chronicles 20:15 KJV. Most people think the battle is physical, or is played from the outside of what you see. The battle is always on the inside of you. It is never what is around you or the obstacles that you see with your physical eyes: it is always what you see with your third eye, your conscious. *You can control your emotions, or you can let your emotions control you.* Even though you are dealing with other people, your actions dictate whether you win or lose. People think they have to fight the battle with their own power, fighting with their emotions. For some odd reason we think we are more powerful than God. You cannot defeat the

Devil by yourself, no matter how hard you try. The situation may look like a situation you think you can handle. You may think, *Yeah, I got this*, and respond in a weak way that you may believe was a strong way. You may even win the battle through your own power, but in God's eyes you lost, because that wasn't even your battle to be fighting in the first place. You may beat someone in a fistfight because they did something to you, and on top of that they were feeble. Your confidence was sky-high, and you just had to exhibit your power to teach that person a lesson. That was a small Devil you encountered in your eyes. How did that make you better? That wasn't even a challenge, but your self-esteem was so low, you had to respond to feel good about yourself. You won the battle on the outside but lost on the inside. You may even feel the need to prove yourself to people that what they say about you or do to you is wrong. You didn't create yourself, so why explain or prove yourself? The Devil made you look ignorant. You thought that the other person was the enemy, but what you didn't realize was that you are your own enemy. Godly people reserve their power for a battle that produces positivity or growth in some form, something that makes you a better, stronger person. Sometimes you lose when you respond.

No Response is the Best Response.

What would you do if someone called you out of your name? What would you do if someone talked to you all types of crazy? Would you take the bait and respond like a worldly person would? I understand that sometimes you may have to respond, because you are human, and at the end of the day, we are all worldly to some extent. You have to elevate yourself above a worldly point of view and understand that what a person does or says to you really doesn't exist. Once their words leave their tongue and hit the air, they vanish. Their words are dead once they leave their mouth. When you do let their behavior exist in your world, that is when you stoop to their level, which is self-defeating. You are better than that. What you don't say or don't do in the presence of adversity speaks more loudly than what you could have done. *"A fool's wrath is presently known: but a prudent man covereth shame"—Proverbs 12:16 KJV.* How do you define being wise? Being wise is being able to discern what is true or right. What does discern mean? To discern means to see or recognize something that is not clear. When something is not clear, it means that it is foggy, hard to see. In actuality, to be wise is to have the ability to see past all the bullshit into what is really going on. When it is not clear, that is all the bullshit that you see with your two physical eyes. When it is clear after the fog, you see with your God Eye, the eye inside of your head, your conscious. *The God eye shows you the real, and the physical eye shows you the fake.*

Take the time to look past the fog before you respond. Do not respond to insults, judgments, negativity, or any other form of abuse. Once you get past the fog as to what was said or done to you, you will realize that the fog was their insecurities, low self-esteem, hurt, and unresolved grief, anger, confidence, or fear. It could be all types of personal issues. They take their pain out on other people. Their life gets foggier and foggier, and you are not able to see the real them within the fog. Seeing the fog in their life will lead you to see how worthless a response is. Your response wouldn't get past the fog in their life, so it doesn't do you or them any good. The fog in their life makes them blind to recognize the real that's being presented by you; which is not responding. Responding to negativity fogs up your life, and the real you get hidden. A response to negativity is using 90 percent of our power and 10 percent of God's power; and that is always a loss. *Responding to the devil is always a lose-lose situation, even if you are right.* That is the same as being 90 percent physical, and 10 percent mental. *"Every prudent man dealeth with knowledge: but a fool layeth open his folly." —Proverbs 13:16 KJV.* When someone insults you, you don't have to say anything back. The power is yours, so don't give it away. The game is to be played from a 90 percent mental, 10 percent physical aspect. The mental part comes from listening to God, and the physical part comes from doing our part.

90 Percent Mental & 10 Percent Physical

The game is played above the shoulders. The mind does most of the work, while the body gets the credit. Before the body, it was the soul, which was God. God-the-soul, directs our mind, and our mind directs our body. The soul directing our mind is the 90 percent mental, and the mind directing the body is the other 10 percent, and when you add both together, you get a 100 percent, which is God all together. The body is just the obedient organ of the cycle. The body is the outward source on the outside that defines what is going on the inside. If the mind says do this first then that second, then this third, your body is going to do the exact same in that order. Without your mind, the body has no safety net. Nothing that cares about it or guides it. The body will do whatever. The man wears the clothes; the clothes don't wear the man. The clothes are just doing what they're told, and the man is telling the clothes what to do. That is why the body is only 10 percent, because they are just obeying. Nothing more, nothing less. The body has no sense of embarrassment or feelings, because it is not able to control itself. The body only cares about what you make it care about. The body shouldn't care about anything, because it is not who we really are. *The less your mouth says, the more your body does.* See your body is only 10 percent, so why put any percentage higher on your body. Don't put more on your body than you can back up. You know the saying, "Don't write checks that your ass can't cash."

Without God, the mind doesn't exist. On earth, the mind and God are in a relationship, or "they should be", and God is the leader in the relationship, so to speak. You know how when you submit your vows people say 'til death do us part. They say those words, because when one is dead, it is disconnected from the other, and since our mind is a part of our body, then it is disconnected from God when we die. During our earthly relationship, God is the leader of the mind. He tells the mind what it is capable of doing and what it's not capable of doing. Without God, the mind wouldn't tell the body anything, and the body would suffer the consequences. God will direct your mind as to what's best. God gives your soul faith, and your soul gives it to the mind, and that same faith is transferred to the body. See, God created a soul and put certain things into one to do. That in which makes our soul divine, since we weren't put here to be good at everything, only what God designed us to be good at. We are not supposed to get involved in everything or be around everything. Our soul only has faith in the things that God created it to have faith in, while sometimes the mind will lie and create false faith in the body. The mind will tell the body to do things that it was never created to do. Without God, the mind is full of pride, ego, selfishness, deceit, fear, shame, and disbelief. We have to put our mind on the things God says to put our mind on. He says to have confidence, strength, truth, light, humbleness, unselfishness, and faith. Once our mind follows God, so will the body. The mind becoming 90 percent mental comes from the relationship that the mind has with God. When the mind and God are on one accord, then you will be able to exhibit the 90 percent mental. You now have more in you than on you, and when it is in you, it speaks for itself. That is God speaking for you. You now have less to prove and more to exhibit. Believe me when I say this—people may act like your lack of a response was still a loss, but deep down they know the truth. When you win on the inside, you automatically win on the outside.

Don't Judge, for Your Eyes May Deceive You

Just like I said in an earlier chapter of how I may have looked low to the cashier because I was sticking to the code within my financial means, it wasn't what it looked like. That is why you shouldn't judge people or look down on them, because you never know their reasons. Everything is not what it looks like. There are broke real people, and rich fake people. Not judging people and keeping your opinions to yourself makes God happy. He's happy to see that you are keeping it G. *"Therefore thou art inexcusable, o man, whosoever thou art that judgest: for wherein thou judgest another, thou condemnest thyself; for thou that judgest doest the same things"—Romans 2:1 KJV.* When we say something about what someone else does, we are only talking about what we do. It is like exposing the man in the mirror, which is ourselves. I realize that when I don't judge people, I have a good conscious about my sins, and they don't bother me, but when I do judge other people, my spirit bothers me. God will allow what you said about someone to reveal itself in your life, just to show you that your soul is no different from any other soul. A voice in me may say, "You are only talking about yourself," or my conscious may show me something I do in comparison to what I said about someone else. I may do the same thing just in a different way. If a person knew who they were, what their code was, or what they stood for, they would be at peace with themselves, knowing God made all of us different. When you are at peace with yourself, then it allows you to be at peace with everyone else. Let them live, allow people to be able to be themselves. Don't turn up your nose at anyone. They say, "The things that people do that bother you are exactly the same things that bother you about yourself." That is what "they" say, though, don't take my word for it, I am just the messenger.

Even though I don't support strippers, robbing, killing, dating outside your race, or other things, it doesn't mean I am not able to adapt or be around them. I can relax and talk to them like they're everyday people. I'm not able to down play anyone's lifestyle. *A person of understanding understands even when he or she doesn't understand.* I have had reasons why I do some of the things I do, so I understand not understanding, and the best way to understand someone is to listen. Even if you don't respond to them, listening will do wonders for someone. I remember times when I misjudged someone until I heard their story, and hearing their story made me feel like a fool for speaking so quickly about them. *"Wherefore, my beloved brethren, let every man be swift to hear, slow to speak, slow to wrath: - James 1:19 KJV.*

Show No Favoritism

Do you show favoritism to the things that you consider little in life? Things like the clothes or shoes you got? Or do you just leave your clothes and shoes when new clothes or shoes come out? Do you even clean your shoes? Do you treat that little rundown car you got like BMW, or do you just treat it like a rundown car? Do you treat that $100 you have like it could possibly be $10,000 one day, or do you just look at it like it's $100? God looks at all of that. Ask yourself, how do you treat the people in life that are not important to you? Sticking to God's code of not showing favoritism to people includes treating your enemy like a friend, treating that poor man the same way you would treat a man who can hire you. Treating someone's mother like you would treat your mother. You have to be solid all the way around. To God, your mother and that person on the street with nowhere to stay are equal. Her being your mother doesn't mean anything to God other than your respecting, protecting, and honoring her. Everyone is equal to Him, and should be equal to you also. If you want to define your relationship to all God's people, try treating someone who is not on your level as if they were on your level. Treat them as if they had just as much money as you or were your best friend. God doesn't want us to treat people as the person they are. He wants us to treat them as if they can be more than what they are. Why treat a drug addict like a drug addict? Then they will always be a drug addict. Treat that drug addict better than they treat themselves. Maybe, one day they will allow the love you give them to work in their lives, and it may motivate them to stop doing drugs.

Now, if people really have the faith like they say they do, then they could be optimistic in seeing the potential being brought out of someone by how they treat the other person. People tend to stay the same in life and not become better because people treat them as if all hope is gone out of their life. We sometimes may walk around prejudging people by their outside situation without knowing that it is greatness in everyone. You're telling a person that they are better than they are, or getting on their ass is good motivation. You are feeding positive energy into their life. Do not accept people's situation. Your lifting them up may be the spark they need to believe in themselves once again. *"Death and life are in the power of the tongue: and they that love it shall eat the fruit thereof" – Proverbs 18:21 KJV*. Speak life into people: "You are better than that," "Get up off your ass and do something," "You are a queen/king, why are you treating yourself this way?" "Pick your head up," "You are not who the world sees you as."

Honesty

You have to be honest with people. If God shows you something about someone, and they ask you about it, then tell them exactly how you feel. Give constructive criticism. People already feel a certain way about themselves, but they just want someone to tell them about themselves to confirm it. People are looking for it. The God in them is looking for it. What I am about to say may sound bad, but it's the best way to be. *Stop caring about people's feelings; right is right no matter how you or someone else may feel.* Caring about their feelings will hurt you, and it will definitely hurt them. Honesty doesn't have feelings; the words "honesty" and "feelings" don't like each other. If you really care about someone, then you are not going to care if they get upset about something you said. Sticking to the code does not involve feelings, just principles that you will live and die by. Now we all have feelings and want to see people happy, but we have to remember that it's not about them, or me, but God and His code. God says, *"Open rebuke is better than secret love"-Proverbs 27:5 KJV.* That means rejecting, denying, or telling someone "no" is better than lying about it or holding it in. That can weigh heavy on your heart; that is why God says, *"Be ye angry, and sin not: let not the sun go down upon your wrath:"— Ephesians 4:26 KJV.* Honesty doesn't mean you are right, but it does confirm that you're not wrong, either. You are only wrong when you don't say anything. You could be wrong and still open someone's eyes to your point of view. Before, they didn't see the situation from your point of view; now they do, even though your honesty was the wrong answer. Their view is broader now because of your opinion. Your honesty will open new doors in their brains and connect missing pieces of the puzzle in them. You have now helped them complete a puzzle in their life. They now understand that the things they exhibit are not viewed in the way they thought. Their view of the situation shows them that everybody doesn't see things the way they do. I remember a time when I felt like my friend was neglecting me, and I told them. Come to find out, it wasn't even what I thought it was. Even though I was wrong, my honesty opened up his subconscious. What I thought was going on could've being going on inside of them subconsciously without them knowing. That part of his subconscious is now aware of itself.

Loyalty

(Being loyal starts with being loyal to God, and being loyal to God is not going to always make the ones around you happy. Be careful not to confuse loyalty with emotions; thinking that things are always supposed to agree with your feelings, or the feelings of people around you. For example: your friend is not supposed to tell you what your significant other is doing when you are not around. God will do that.)

Loyalty means having an allegiance to someone or something. That means I gave all my trust, love, support, and life to them. When you are loyal to someone, their pain is your pain, and their life is your life. They put all their trust in you not to betray them, and vice versa. It is up to you to choose who you will die for. You have to be willing to give your life for someone to show ultimate loyalty, so before you say you are loyal to someone, ask yourself, "Will I lose my life to save theirs?" Loyalty goes all out; it doesn't care about the consequences. *"A man that hath friends must shew himself: and there is a friend that sticketh closer than a brother" – Proverbs 18:24 KJV.* You are not able to be loyal to everyone, and everyone is not able to be loyal to you. Pick and choose who you give your loyalty too. Loyalty does not come in big packs. Loyalty is not formed from a big group of people. They say less is more, so a close friend may be more loyal to you then the rest of your family, or the whole world. That friend will make up for all the disloyalty that other people may have shown you. For you to be loyal to someone, there would have to be some shared pain applied behind you all. Love will have had to grow between you all. You all are so close that you all are one, so what hurts them, hurts you. You all share every type of pain together. There is no in between in the pain you all share. You are also by that person's side no matter the situation or circumstance. You may not agree, but you stick by their side.

Stay True

Most people only talk about being loyal and honest when everything is good. You shouldn't only be loyal, or any other good thing in life, only when it has been good to you. *"For if ye love them which love you, what thank have ye? For sinners also love those that love them. And if ye do good to them which do good to you, what thank have ye? For sinners also do even the same. And if ye lend to them of whom ye hope to receive, what thank have ye? For sinners also lend to sinners, to receive as much again"- Luke 6:32-34 KJV.* Most people in the universe, and even I at times, have got caught up in only doing what has been done to us. We may get credit from the world for doing what has been done to us, but we will get no credit from God. God knows that doing good for good is as easy as it comes. There is no challenge in being real around real people. There is no challenge in being honest around people who like honesty. There is no challenge in being loyal to people who have been loyal to you. I am not saying that you are supposed to be all jolly jolly with a person after they have betrayed you, but you are still supposed to act the same way to them as if everything is all good, even when you know it's not. What I mean by that is don't let anyone's dishonesty, or disloyalty, or bad deeds toward you affect your loyalty or honesty toward them. If a friend lies to you or betrays you in a certain type of way; you shouldn't bash them, look down on them, or be in your feelings about what they did to you, no matter what it may be. You shall continue to keep all their secrets, not judge them, and not talk about them to new friends or family. I know something's hurt to the point to where you feel as if you have to talk about it to someone, or get revenge, or cancel all loyalty and honesty toward them because of their mistake. Little do you know to God you still have to hold your end of the bargain and continue to be loyal and honest to them. I have felt victim to this type of thinking and decision-making in different types of way. I am going to lie to you, because you lie to me. I am going to do you wrong, because you did me wrong. I am going to look down on you, because you betrayed me. I am going to say, "fuck you," because you said "fuck me." I am not going to ever lend you money again, because you didn't repay me. The things I just said are not the right way to go about handling betrayal. It just shows that the loyalty didn't come from the heart. We were just as good to the other person as they were to us. *Don't only do when it has been done, and don't only give when it has been given.*

Who are we to get tied up in our emotions because of how someone has treated us? We are not God. In his eyes, we are all fucked up people! In some form or fashion, we deserve the things that happen to us, because whether you believe it or not, we have all been dishonest, disloyal, or have done something evil to someone. We are just as equal to the person who betrayed us. We owe God, and a part of really doing good is doing good to those who do bad to you. God doesn't care about doing good for good: there is no lasting realness in that to him.

"But love ye your enemies, and do good, and lend, hoping for nothing again; and your reward shall be great, and ye shall be the children of the highest: for he is kind unto the unthankful and to the evil. Be ye therefore merciful, as your father also is merciful"- Luke 6:35-36 KJV. Start, or continue, to do good even when evil is present. You may not get worldly rewards or the credit you think you deserve, but God is noticing all the pain you endure. Lasting character is created from adversity.

Chapter Six
Unlocking Women: You Are His World

WHEN I THINK of the word *woman*, I think of the "wo" part of the word that plays a part in the word *womb*. The definition of womb is the place of origination, where something is created. When creating something, you need a nice space, a good environment, a good vibe, cleanliness, pureness, protection, patience, and organization to plant the seed. How do you expect a seed to grow well if it is disturbed or lacking vital needs? Women are the most vital source for life on earth, but if you all are lacking in certain areas of patience, temper, cleanliness of the body and spirit, self-esteem, self-worth, and self-respect, how do you expect to create anything within you, or why would anybody else want to create anything within you, from your soul, mind, or body?

The code of the woman is the second greatest code a man could unlock, unlocking himself being the greatest.

First, a man has to have a reason to unlock you. No man wants to plant any kind of seed inside of a woman with no code to herself, whether it is physical, mental, or spiritual. Why unlock you if you have no lock? There is no telling who or what has been inside of a woman with no lock. I want the seed I plant to have the right nurturing; any other real man would want the same. A woman could have things coming and going out her life back-to-back, from men, mental disturbances (better known as mind games), bitterness, abuse, sex, and all other type of bullshit that comes with life. Make sure my seed is secure and not being poisoned or disturbed. A seed needs room, quietness, pureness, proteins, nurturing, healthiness, and neatness to grow.

A seed of any sort shouldn't be dysfunctional, and manipulated into something it wasn't meant to be. Before God can lock the code to a woman's nature, and before a man can unlock a woman's nature, she has to clean out her soil.

Gather Your Emotions

Do you all know the definition of the word *hoe*? A hoe is an agricultural tool used for digging. Like most people when using a shovel to dig, they are digging and looking for something there. A lot of women have been letting men dig in them, whether it is mental, physical, or spiritually looking for something that isn't there, whether it be love, happiness, or self-esteem. Letting them dig in you, trying to find something that isn't really there. Only God can place those things within a woman, and really God has already placed those things there. Women just think they need a man to dig it out of them. Women think a man is going to find it, and that's why they allow them to dig in them. What makes women think a man can find something in them that they have yet to find in themselves?

The shovel is for her, and not the man is what she doesnt realize. A man is not able to dig if a woman doesn't give him the shovel. He is not able to find what they are looking for while they are letting him dig in them. Only God can do that.

In my experience *situational women are emotional women*. Emotions in this case is nothing more than what your body wants and your soul doesn't need. What I am saying adds up the same in situations that I have encountered with women. I remember being at the Kwanzaa Fest in Dallas, Texas, and getting a young lady's number. Then I remember being at the fair a year later and getting that young lady's number again. Apparently, she didn't remember me from the first time, just based on the vibe we had the second time, or maybe she did. Vibe is another meaning for spiritual connection, or energy. Even though she didn't remember who I was, the vibe was the same, the situation was the same, so it didn't matter who I was, as long as the situation was the same. There was nothing different about me; I had not progressed in any area of life. I didn't make any progress, and neither did she…apparently. She was still acting off emotions, and *emotions get you zero progress*. As long as the situation fit her emotions, she was for it. That is a lot of females today. As long as the situation fits their emotions, then anything can happen. It doesn't matter the man that she come in contact with, if she is still acting off emotions, then she will get the same results. That is not good for a female. Most females' emotions are all over the place.

Different face, same case. Basically, say a different male approaches her, but she ends up getting the same results. It was a different guy, but the same type of guy. That is what emotions get you. Let's say a woman start with 6. But let her emotions lead her actions, then when it's all said and done, she will still end up with 6. That is zero progress. The same type of men will continue to approach her and receive her attention if she doesn't put her emotions on the back burner.

Stop Hiding

"Jesus saith unto her, go, call thy husband, and come hither. The woman answered and said, I have no husband. Jesus said unto her, thou hast well said, I have no husband: for thou hast had five husbands; and he whom thou now hast is not thy husband: in that saidst thou truly"—John 4:16-18 KJV. Her body language and spirit told Jesus how many men she had slept with. Now that is Jesus, so of course He knows everything, but a man also has the discernment to read a woman before He even approaches her. Since a man is not God or Jesus, he won't see everything they see, but when they see you, he should see *a woman that is unable to be figured out*. All he need to know is that you are a woman

worth discovering, and his discernment will tell him that. No matter how much a man discovers, he stills come up short of discovering the woman, because a woman of God grows every day, so therefore she cannot be fully discovered. That is why women need to become a whole new woman and let God lock them just to unlock them God is going to lock the caterpillar woman and unlock the butterfly woman.

A lot of women hide themselves behind womanly clothes, college degrees, money, independent status, beauty, etc. They believe all these possessions make them a woman worth approaching. None of those things can hide her worth or how she really feels about herself. See, she has all these things, but to acquire those things doesn't require a development in character for the most part. It may make one feel elevated, but in reality the only thing that was elevated was their ability to hide their self-esteem. One's status and possessions paint a false reality; their own life deceives them. Making them think you are somebody who in reality doesn't even exist. Ask yourself these questions: What has progressed on the inside? How do I really feel? Is my spirit the same?

See, when a man reads a woman, he reads them from the inside, not the outside. Nothing in their possession makes them look better than they really are. For example, before a woman had a degree, she was deceitful, and now that she has that degree, she still thinks deceitfully. This is simply because going to college and getting a degree doesn't make a woman better for God. All that does is challenge their intelligence, and intelligence and character are totally two different things. I have known females who were whores with deceitful ways in high school or college, but now that they are going to college or graduating college they feel as if they can hide their true whorish spirit, or men will let them get away with their deceitful thoughts and behavior. They are not a new woman; they are just in a new situation: you are situational. The evil about the whole situation is that some of them may use their possessions to intentionally or unintentionally deceive a man. Possessions can be a beautiful face, or body, a beautiful bank account, a job, or a lifestyle. Women figure he may overlook who they really are, because of what they have.

What women fail to realize is that God created woman from the rib of man. Women are a part of men, and that is a reason *why men know women better than women know themselves*. All humans have the God-like intuition that allows them to see beyond what is not seen. Women wonder why the results they get from men when they didn't have anything are the same results they get from men they have everything. *You may look like a woman, but do you have the spirituality of a woman?*

Goddess's Time

God doesn't revolve around humans; humans revolve around God. People in general think they can do whatever they want, when they want, and then when they are ready to do what is right, the world is supposed to align with them. God should always be your road map, not the other way around. You know like they say, you snooze, you lose. If you women are not paying attention, and only thinking about yourself, then you may miss out on a blessing in a man. Women spend so much time doing what they wanted to do without involving God. They now think they can now bullshit their way to a good, healthy relationship. It doesn't work like that. You know how people think— just because they're young, they can just do whatever, and everything will eventually end up working their way. That is a self-deceiving theory.

There are women who spend their younger days just getting themselves together physically, financially, etc. Don't focus on the desires of the world first then focus on the desires of God last; life doesn't work like that. I know a lot of people's parents from generation to generation used this same saying, "Date someone that is doing something with their lives, or in college, or on your level." I have heard that saying so many times. Now women, I am not saying by any means get a man that is not able to provide. I agree with the saying in a sense, but it's like they are telling you to put lifestyle first and character and spirit last. Yeah, it's cool to the world for a woman to marry someone that makes just as much money as she does, or has a college degree like she does, can do more of what they want more than another man can, or is on whatever level they claim to be on, but it is fake to God.

A lot of women and men lose because of that mindset. I have ridden the bus and train to work week to week with the same clothes. The clothes were clean, and I wasn't a bum. I know most women would prejudge me as if I weren't on their level. Little do they know, I had money, but I was investing in myself. I put my spirit, soul, and dreams above all. I'd seen the bigger picture. Do you as a women see the bigger picture? Don't put what a man has or doesn't have at the moment or in general over his spirit. Also, women don't put what you have or don't have over your spirit. If you put yourself first and put God last, you end up with nothing. What women don't realize is that while they were doing them, and not merely focusing on the more spiritual aspects of life that God would like them to focus on, they were just creating a fire that they would one day have to walk through. Don't do what is supposed to be first, last, and vice versa. Focus on the spirit first, and the possessions and accomplishments last.

Women should think about when they were just having fun, doing whatever fun is in your eyes: were you creating images of your self-worth, lowering your value as a woman? Like I said earlier in the chapter, a man can read a woman's spirit.

Every time a woman runs into a man, I don't care how he makes her feel; if he is a man with a relationship with God, then he will be aware of all her deceitful ways. When I say a man has relationship with God; I am not saying he goes to church every Sunday, or read the bible every day, but I am saying that he stays in close connection with God.

Women are not able to hide from God. Then the woman who mainly focused on herself doesn't even know how to relate with a man with anything other than her assets. Her happiness comes from a false image of materialistic things. What she doesn't realize is that when she begins dating is that her possessions or accomplishments do the dating for her. The real her is hidden by what she has. She will unintentionally judge a man by what he has instead of who he is without even knowing she is doing so. Her money or car will pick her men for her. They will tell her whether a man is fit to have her. It won't be her that will be doing the picking; it will be her lifestyle. *She didn't make the money, cars, degrees, beauty, intelligence. The money, cars, beauty, intelligence, and degrees made her.* Basically, she is nothing without them. Who is she, really? If she lost it all today, would she still have confidence in herself? Would she even know where to start with getting into a relationship? Would she even know what to look for in a man, besides what he has to offer? Her whole life was, or still is, false. Some women may be where they are supposed to be with the world, but they are nowhere near where you are supposed to be with God. *God will never have to catch up with our time, but we have to catch up with His.*

No Man Is Better than the Next

Men think that they are the man. All men have an ego big as the universe. I guess you can say that ego stems from testosterone. Men don't want any man invading the territory that is theirs, no matter what it is. I was watching the National Geographic Channel, and there were two mating lions, and when the lion found him a female mate, he would roar to confirm his territory, letting every other lion know that the female lion was his. Just like lions, men want their woman all to themselves and want every other man to know that the woman is theirs. They want to be the only one able to take advantage of their woman. A man having a woman all to himself makes him feel like the king of his jungle. Men want that power, and it is only his power if no other man has accomplished what he has accomplished with her. That is why back in the biblical days when a woman committed adultery or cheated on her man she was looked down upon and treated as if her worth was gone. Basically, it was because God created her body for one man, but that is a whole other topic of its own. The thing I am trying to say is, if *you allow one man to treat you a certain way, then all men will think they can treat you that way*. All men are equal, and no man is going to allow himself to feel lower than another man. If a woman is going to make it easy for one man; she has to make it easy for all men. Women nowadays tend to allow some men to get away with things that they wouldn't let another man get away with. A woman may let one man get all your attention and make another man work for it. She may allow one man to disrespect her, or make her worth feel lower, and then make another man treat her like a queen. That is playing both sides; either be on one side or the other, there is no in between. *"A double minded man is unstable in all his ways"- James 1:8 KJV*. Don't make it easy on some men and hard on others. I understand that a woman may like the man that she make it easy on a little more than the other man or men. He may have money, fame, status, attractiveness, etc. Then the man that she made it hard for may be the exact opposite of everything I just named. Get out of a sheet of paper and create a list of principles that you would live by with all men, no exceptions. These principles have to be the same for every man: good or bad, rich or poor, attractive or unattractive, your type or not your type. Be solid to your principles. *Be the same to all men* because, even if you aren't, you will still get the same results from all men. A woman then may wonder how can a man she is not even attracted to treat her like she is nothing. The answer is she wasn't solid to herself.

When playing both sides and lower standards for men is when a woman loses. Even the men a woman may not really like will treat her the same way. Even if she lowers them for one man, all men will still treat her the same, good or bad. God will let a man know if a woman is 50 percent deceitful and 50 percent truthful. Why would a man pay for something that his brother received for free? It doesn't get that good little momma.

Stop Seeking Attention

Those who are heard are not seen, and those who are seen are not heard. I am currently reading another book at the moment, and I just so happen to have stumbled across some insight. The book was talking about how on our spiritual journey, we should avoid "getting attached" to people because it leads to a control drama, mainly in male and female relationships. The book says how when you meet someone of the opposite gender, and you all hit it off really good, and you all are texting, calling each other, and just enjoying each other's company. You may start to like this man, he makes you laugh and treats you right, and you see a future with him. In the book it says this vibe will eventually die down, and then there will be a control for energy (In reality for an overall understanding; energy is power). You all hit it off strong, and now someone is trying to get control for power, kind of like a two-headed dragon. The woman wants things to go her way, and now the man wants things to go his way. You all are trying to get control for power, and someone is going to lose. Women may start doing things like not texting him first to see if he is going to text first. Women may stop calling him first to see if he is going to call first. The conversations start to change with him, because the woman doesn't want to make it seem like she is losing. Whether women know it or not, they are trying to take his energy away from him so they can be in control.

The book says we have this control drama in our day-to-day life without knowing it. I call it "playing games." The book states that the drama starts because neither male nor female is complete with themselves—they are both insecure—so they subconsciously take energy from the opposite sex to feel complete. The ways that females do these things is by posting certain pictures on social media or saying or doing certain things that they know men want to see and hear to get energy from them, and as soon as a man bites the bait is when he loses his energy. In reality, a female only posted the picture on social media, or dressed the way they dressed, or did whatever they did, to get his energy, because they are not complete within themselves. In some cases of this controlled energy drama, the man just wants to have sex, and the woman just want attention. Either the woman is going to let him have sex and lose, or he is going to give her the attention she wants and lose. Females play all type of different attention games.

For example, women may post pictures on social media, wear certain clothes, say or do subliminal things, etc. Those things are good if they are sincere. Some females may even have a thousand unread messages in their phone, just so they can feel important. Then once they all get the attention they desire in that particular form, then it is on to get the next man's attention. Have you ever sought to get a man's attention, and then when he gave it to you, you didn't want it anymore? You may have felt like you won. It is funny how when people finally get something they want, and then all of a sudden they don't want it any more.

"How can ye believe, which receive honour one of another, and seek not the honour that cometh from God only?"- John 5:44 KJV. Since they are only not one-hundred-percent sure about themselves, they go about seeking attention from other dudes to complete themselves instead of getting it from God. If women didn't have a social media account, or play the little bullshit games they play, would they feel complete? Why don't they have the energy they need? Why are women preying on men to feed their insecurities? Doing things to get attention will go nowhere

on an empty spirit. Those one hundred likes on Facebook or Instagram and fifty unread messages are all cool until reality kicks in. Women allow God to fill your spirit, to become secure within yourselves. Then women won't have to live each day holding their guard up against men with games, because God will be the guard. Now, I do understand that all women need and want attention. Attention is what men should give women, but women have to learn how to naturally receive attention.

Women, become aware of the games and cut them off, because you women are only playing with yourselves in the end. God needs to be a woman's one and only until they are fully in tuned with themselves and become complete, because women are only going around stealing energy that doesn't last, because in reality their self-esteem is not where it is supposed to be. To add on to that, if you women are stealing energy, then most likely your energy is getting stolen also. Continue to fuck over men, and other men will continue to fuck you. Literally!

Get Naked for God

Women have been hiding behind their emotions, independence, favoritism, selfishness, and the attention they receive. As long as they allow those things to lead their life, people will be blind to who the real them is. Women will only attract and receive fakeness from people, because that is who they are. The men they come into contact will be hiding behind a false image also. Men and women will both be deceiving each other in all type of ways. Only the things on the outside of both of them will attract you to each other. Women have all these things protecting them, denying their soul access to flourish. They should let God take that protection them. Take off those clothes and hop in the shower with God. Take off those clothes; in this case, clothes resemble the money, jewelry, clothes, car, status, makeup, attention from men, false self- esteem, and other possessions that they possess such as beauty and attention they received. Don't hide no longer; just look at the shower as the personal Heaven where God is cleaning. The water being running represents God washing the relationship with all those things out and off of the body, mind, and vagina. Now air-dry; not drying like the world dry's. Stand there and let God do the air-drying. There is no towel needed to dry you women. The air represents God's spiritual time with the woman. He dry's according to His timing. When women realize that they are dry is when God presents them to the world as being naked. The nakedness represents everything from earlier in the chapter that God has washed off. The naked woman is the real woman. A woman being naked to the world is going to make her feel embarrassed, only because the real her is visible to the world. No more hiding. She is going to feel uncomfortable, but it is allowing the worldly, emotional, situational, and fleshly woman in her not to exist. You know how shocked you would be if you saw a naked person outside in broad daylight. It would shock you and it would have everybody staring. That is how men will look at the woman's soul. That is how they will look on a day-to-day basis. The men who once approached that woman will be scared to approach that woman. The men who treated her badly will be scared to treat her badly. They are speechless as to how to approach her. To them that is a woman they never seen before, but to the woman that is just the woman in them that the world has yet to meet. She has a priceless confidence, self-worth, and self-esteem. She is just glowing everywhere she goes, walking with high energy and positive vibes. The elevated new woman is going to shock every man that sees her head up. (That woman may be you). These blessings and more will happen that I am not even able to comprehend myself. Women do not cover yourselves up or go back to those same things God took off or out of you; let your soul glow: he locked the old you for a reason. God has some clothes for you that fit only you, protect only you, and cherish only you. Those clothes are your soul mates in every area of your life. Things that only fit you. When you put them on, they will never come off. I'm talking about physical clothes, mental clothes, and spiritual clothes. Your clothes, hair, self-esteem, confidence, self-worth, etc. The way you walk, talk, market yourself, show your purpose—everything in your life will come from Heaven.

Chapter Seven
Unlocking Men: Finding Her in Your Soul

"*BUT LET EVERY man prove his own work, and then shall he have rejoicing in himself alone, and not in another. For every man shall bear his own burden*"-Galatians 6:4-5 KJV. Don't think you are supposed to get the same results with a woman just as another man may receive. You are not him, and that is neither a bad thing nor good thing. It is exactly what it is; *you are not him, and he isn't you.* What he can do, you are not able to, and what you can do, he may not be able to do. A lot of men fail to be their own man, or the best man they can be, because of comparisons. I personally believe that *our spiritual comparisons to the next man* is one of our biggest losses to women. We want to have sex with a woman just a fast as the next man. We will treat a female we adore like a whore because the next man did, not necessarily because that is how we really felt: we don't won't to feel lame and such. When it comes to women, or to life in general, we as men have a monkey see, monkey do disease. Whether we want to admit it or not, we want to be the man above the man. Instead of being our own man. If we are not in first place compared to every other man, then we are losing to ourselves; even though that is not right, that is how we think. Little do we know is that we are supposed to only be in first place with ourselves. If us men only compared ourselves to ourselves, then we would be parallel to God's plan. We should only worry about how we compare to ourselves rather than comparing ourselves to other men. That is why most men are never at peace with themselves when it comes to dealing with women, because they are most likely trying to keep up with the next man. We will never be able to get the results of the next man. He can accomplish something you are not able to with a female, and another dude is not able to accomplish something else with a female that you can accomplish. *You lose a woman when you follow another man's game plan.* As you can see, it is nothing but a revolving cycle. I can do what he's not able to do, and he can do what I'm not able to do. Do not think that because the next man accomplished something with a female in a time above you, that that makes him better than you. Race your race, because if you race his race, you will never win. Use your God-given speed to determine the timing with which you operate.

God's Time

You know as a man we have two brains. We have that brain in our jeans that hang low and we have that brain on our shoulders. The one on our shoulders tends to have more sense than the one in our jeans when it comes to women. The one on our shoulders tells us to have more self-control, while the other tells us to go for it all. The one on our shoulders tells us to be patient, while the other wants it now. The one on our shoulders knows how to treat a woman, while the other doesn't care about a woman. That head just wants to get a nut, or ejaculation as the correct way to refer to, and go on about his business. The one on our shoulders will tell a woman what she needs to hear, and the one between our legs will tell a woman what she wants to hear. The one on our shoulders operates from God Time, while the one in our jeans operates from the Devil Time. The God Time is more caring, patient, honest, sincere, and respectful. The Devil Time just doesn't give a damn! It just wants a nut.

I used to be told a lot that my eyes said things that my mouth didn't say. Women used to tell me that my eyes will let them know if I just want to have sex with them or if I really enjoyed their company. I believe that is because my eyes speak for my soul, since I am a naturally spiritual person. My consciousness outweighs all the bullshit I present. That is just how God created me; I'm not speaking for other men as far as that goes. For example, I could be telling a woman that I care for her or I would like to get to know her. These are just examples of what I could have been saying. In reality, I was saying a more advanced version of "caring or liking her" than the examples I gave. I could say those same two things in two different situations, but they would have a different meaning to the two different females. One female would take it in heed that I was being sincere, and the other would take it as bullshit. That is, because she could read my spirit and my energy (or vibe), and it was a fake spirit presenting itself to her. I didn't really like her or seen anything in her but what her body had to offer. Your fake spirit will only win against a fake-spirited female. She has to be just as full of shit as you are.

A God Time will not even approach a female that he doesn't see anything in. A God Time will not approach a female based on just the physical appearance of her body. A God Time uses his insight to determine whether he can approach her. When a God Time sees something it really likes, it sees an adventure that it would like to explore. It sees sand that it would take to the beach. It sees a thousand women in one woman. It doesn't see a price, it sees value and worth. It comes from a place of honesty, sincerity, respect, and patience, and most of all, *a God time doesn't have a motivation.* It comes from the heart, a place of peace. It doesn't see anything that it could gain from the situation, lose, or win. A Devil Time on the other hand will give its last to get a woman's goods. It will say and do whatever it has to do to please itself. A Devil Time only thinks about today and never tomorrow. It doesn't see a soul; it sees a body that it can take control of. Since we as men are on the same team, a Devil Time will make it that much harder for a real man, because what a real man sees is not her presentation to the world. A Devil Time will have a *female thinking she is more than what she is*. She has a big head with small actions. Now her mirror image is deceived by the lies that a man has told her or showed her. Little does she know that she is nowhere: he took her mind, body, or soul. That is when another problem of many arises that we should unlock to avoid.

Don't Drown in Her Ocean

You know how you are about to have sex with a girl, and you know they get a little wet or moist down there, or should I say, they get real wet and moist down there. You pull out your weapon, wood, tool, penis, dick, or whatever you want to call it, gets on hard. All those hormones rush blood to your penis to make it extend, or grow. Now your penis is getting real hard, and you are about to put your penis inside of her vagina. Let's just hypothetically say that when you put your tool inside of her, that it just falls in. Like it doesn't fit or grip because her vagina muscles are too big for your penis muscles; in other words, you are drowning in her ocean. Now, there are all different reasons as to why her muscles are bigger than yours. She could hypothetically be a whore, filled with a lot of penises who have dug a hole in her which opened her muscles. Her walls are all knocked down, and her ocean has no limits. Or on the other hand, you may just be too small, and your boat may not fit her ocean. That is the same for making a female feel like something that she isn't. Men in her previous experiences could have dug a hole in her head to make her feel like something that she isn't. Now here you come in filling her head up even more, making her feel more of nothing with your deceiving words. She's probably heard it all, so now all you do is drown inside her. You and every other man that God didn't create for her are going to just fall right in her. Now your thoughts, lies, and false actions are all a part of her. She is living life based off all the lies that men have told her. Everything about the men in her life is now a part of her. Her life is a big lie based on things said and done to her. You might as well be her child, because you are now inside of her. When she speaks, she is giving birth to the lies you have told her. When she walks, she is giving birth to the false confidence you gave her. When she expects certain results from men, she is giving birth to the results you gave her. Now God has to build her walls back up and remove all the poison from her vagina and her mind that men have put there. God has to now make it fit for the right man to enter into both areas—mind and vagina. Her mind and vagina are a big empty hole. God needs your help, because we as men are the closest image of God that she sees. *He can help women if you help him.*

Lead by Example

Your job to help God is to show women who they really are without telling them who they really are. You have to reverse the damage done to her brain, vagina, and spirit without saying a word. *Without attention, whorish women wouldn't exist.* A woman needs a man's attention in every area of life to feel alive. The attention that was given to her is the reason why she acts the way she acts now. It is the reason why she thinks every man wants her. Stop lying to our women/God's Daughters. Women wouldn't be prostituting on the street or in strip clubs if we didn't give them our money. Women wouldn't use their bodies for attention if we didn't glorify their bodies. Women would know who they really are if we didn't sell them a dream. Women wouldn't wear the clothes they wear if we didn't like their pictures on Instagram or Facebook. *God makes the man accountable for why the woman acts the way she does.* We are responsible for them. It is not their fault that they are the way they are. You remember the story in the Garden of Eden when Adam and Eve ate from the tree of knowledge. *"And the lord God called unto Adam, and said unto him, where art thou?"—Genesis 3:9 KJV.* You see God didn't call Eve's name.

Basically, God asked Adam, "Why weren't you watching her? You are responsible for her." Woman is the representation of Man. Like the condition of your shoes represent you, similar to the cleanliness of your home. It is all the same thing. They wouldn't do any of the self-degrading things they do if it wasn't for us. What God wants us to do as men is to *start ignoring their deceitful ways*. I know all men probably won't stop going to the strip clubs or things of that nature: they're not perfect. What you can do is walk past them like they don't exist. When you see a woman looking for attention by what she has on or on social media, or being loud, dancing, or just giving you a lustful look or a look as to if you know you can get her and take off with her in any form possible, act as if you don't even see her right there. Eventually, if enough men did that to all women and stopped entertaining their egos, women would start looking in the mirror, asking themselves, "What's wrong?" The less we entertain, the more women will be created without you saying a word. The thing is that women need our attention. They are nothing without it. When women see that their whorish or low attention-seeking acts are not working, that is when they will indirectly be led to God. We sold them the truth, and they have no choice but to buy it. See, because giving them attention was blocking them from hearing God's voice, because when no one is on your side, you run to God. Once men stop giving them attention that is not Godly, that is when God creeps in and says something like, "You see why you shouldn't be dressing like that, my daughter? You shouldn't carry yourself in that way, my daughter. You should wear more clothes, my daughter. You should stop doing things for attention, my daughter. You should stop letting men between your legs, my daughter." See us men block a lot of women from God, but as soon as we get out of her way, that is when God can work. The business is God's; we just advertise it.

Treat All Women with the Same Respect

As people living in the world, or just as worldly people, we tend to take people as they come. However, how they are when we meet them is how we treat and respond to them. We really don't read between the lines or anything. I remember my father used to always tell me, "What you do affects everybody." I take that into consideration in my day-to-day life with different situations. Not only do my decisions toward myself affect people, but also my decisions towards others. The way I treat women will have an everlasting effect on them. It is just like a chain reaction. If I treat her badly, she will treat another man badly, and he will treat another woman badly. *The cycle has to stop with you.* The problem is that we treat women based on how they treat themselves. If they are a whore, then we treat them like a whore. That is why the cycle continues. *Treat people better than they treat themselves.* If they don't respect themselves, we should respect themselves for them. For example, open the door for her even if she doesn't want you to or doesn't expect you to. You may be able to give a woman a better outlook on life by respecting her. If you keep treating people as if they are worth more, then one day they will eventually treat themselves the same way, or see themselves the same way you see them. A woman is no better than a whore: they're all equal. Treat the whore just as equal as the woman. I'm talking from the conversation to how you act toward them. A lot of women don't know how to accept being respected, because they are so used to being disrespected. When a woman doesn't accept the respect, remember it is not about them; give it to them anyway. You are just doing your part. You're taking the low to high, the worthless to worthy, and the lesser to greater.

Only God Can Save Her

There is a time in all parents' lives when they have no control over their kids. They may feel like the power is all theirs, and that will not change. Eventually, reality will kick in, and let them know who is in control. I say reality is God in all situations. A child runs away from home, and the parent has done everything to prevent their child from running away from home, but in the end, everything just wasn't enough. God gives us free will, *"See, I have set before thee this day life and good, and death and evil;" Deuteronomy 30:15 KJV."* People have the will to bring death upon themselves or life upon themselves; the choice is theirs. Just as God is our spiritual parent, our physical parent should also give us a choice to choose. Let's just say that parent went out in the streets, found their child, and made them come back. That child only came back because the parent made them, not because they were willing too. The child will only end up running away again, because the parent didn't allow them to exercise their free will. We know our way back home, and so does the child.

I once encountered a dude in college that was dating a young woman who a lot of men knew of in a way that wasn't too pleasant. There was all types of gossip going around about how she does this and that. She was just a loose cannon; from what they were saying. You know like I said earlier. Back in the biblical days when a woman cheated on her husband, the whole community would treat her like she was nothing. She wouldn't get attention or anything; she was looked upon as an outcast. I figured this dude would do her the same way, but instead it seems as if he was trying to prevent her from bringing misery upon herself. What little does he know is that she had already run away from home, figuratively speaking; her heart is not with him. Every time you see her, you see him. He is always up under her, watching her every move, making sure she doesn't do anything whorish. What he doesn't know is he is doing God an injustice and deceiving himself. Yeah, of course while he is all up on her she is Ms. Innocent, but as soon as he's not around, she is back to being who she really is. In her heart, she is a whore, but around you she is a woman.

A bad heart always exposes good deeds. Understand that sometimes people only do things to please you, not because it was really in their heart to do those things. The heart is the center from which everything flows. She may have looked at it as if she was just in college having fun and living life, but in reality she had the heart of a whore. She didn't want to be with one man; she was open to all opportunity. Therefore, he couldn't save her, even if he was a lifeguard, because when it is all said and done, she was just going to hop right back in the water. A man saving a woman from her own misery will not last, because he didn't let her see where her decisions would take her. *You have to set people free in order for them to know that the world cost.* The love you gave to them for free is that same love that the world is going to make them pay for.

The thing that he was telling God with his actions is that he doesn't have faith that everything will work out. That is why he was all over her, because he was scared that the Devil would take her. What makes him think he is stronger than the Devil? The Devil has way more power than a human ever could. *"The lord shall fight for you, and ye shall hold your peace"- Exodus 14:14 KJV.* Don't try to do God's job; only He can truly show her where her actions will lead her. They say experience is the best teacher.

See, God is in her heart, and only He has access to the inside of her soul. That is somewhere where we cannot control anything. Just like God gives us free will, He will let her be a whore and show her the consequences of being a whore. He is not going to stop her from being a whore or doing whatever she wants to do. We would've never known that the stove was hot if we didn't touch it. We can tell a person all day, "Don't do this. Don't do that," but they are going to do it anyway. Only God can show them why they shouldn't do this or that. God is that experience that we don't have the power to offer. All God is telling men to do is to have faith that she will find her way back home. A man with faith will never try to save a woman from her own misery, because he knows that all dogs find their way back home, and most of all he knows her true savior is God. *When she left she was set free, and when she came back she was worth more than diamonds.* God can turn trash into treasure. It was something to throw away;

now it's something to keep. My words to all men is, if a woman returns to you, best believe she will only return better than she was when you set her free. *Man saving her is temporary; God saving her is forever.*

Don't Allow Your Dick to Build Your Self-Esteem

In society, they may often teach you to be a player while you are young, having sex with all the girls. I remember in my teenage years when I really started feeling myself and having sex with females. It was just the natural thing to do. It seems as if every young man was in competition with the next man subconsciously without knowing it. Internally, we all wanted to feel as if we are that guy. From my experience, that feeling only came when I had sex with a new female. Every female I had sex with gave me more power within myself, or so I thought. Then after I had sex with her, I would have to go tell one of my friends, because, subconsciously, I wanted to be rewarded by him with a pat on the back telling me I did a good job. I wanted to feel as if I was the man by the glory of another man. I was young and didn't realize what picture I was actually painting of myself.

"He that goeth about as a talebearer revealeth secrets: therefore meddle not with him that flattereth with his lips"- Proverbs 20:19 KJV. A lot of men that don't feel secure about themselves will go around always telling their friends who they have had sex with. Now, I understand that you may tell somebody—none of us is perfect—but that is not a pass to do it, because it really doesn't matter

at the end of the day. Now your friend asking you have you had sex with a female is a different story. I remember when I was in college, everyone knew who everyone was having sex with. Every man was telling on themselves, me included. That is just how low our self-esteem was without us actually acknowledging it. What is it that makes us feel good about how many women we have had sex with? We are taught that the more females you have sex with, the more of a man you are.

One day, it hit me that I was guilty of low self-esteem, when my friend came and told me of a young woman that he had just had sex with. At that time, I was becoming aware of it, so in my mind I am saying, "Why are you telling me like I care? I don't care." He seemed excited and happy to tell me at the moment. I slowly realized that it is like a friend is always running to me to tell me of new women he had just had sex with, but why? I realized that I was somebody that was having sex with other women also, so it would only be right to tell a rival of your victory to make yourself feel higher than them. I say that because I am pretty sure he wasn't telling another male virgin that he just had sex with another female. He knows that is useless and wouldn't feed his ego.

As I thought about it, I began to feel used, because it seemed as if my friend was trying to gain praise from me. He wanted me to say "good job" or give him glory or something like that. I say to myself, "Damn! I have been doing my friends like that also without even knowing it." Most men do these things to each other. We seek praise from other men because we do not feel complete about ourselves. A man who feels complete probably wouldn't say anything. Little do we know is that we walk around lacking energy, so we subconsciously steal it from each other. Now I am getting to the message that I am really trying to convey.

Previously, in the chapter about women, I spoke about how they try to take energy from men by gaining attention from them. Now I am going to talk about how men try to take energy from women by having sex with them. Now, a man that is not complete will not feel good about taking a woman on dates, and things of that nature, without expecting to receive something in return. The man doesn't want to feel played, just like the woman doesn't want to feel played. A man can have a hundred yards with a woman, but if he doesn't score a touchdown, then it was all worthless, because in his eyes he lost. A man getting inside the most precious part of a woman's body gives him all the power. Since men have been taught that the more women he has sex with the more power he has, he preys after women. See, after each woman, his energy goes up, but after a while it comes back down, and now he is incomplete again. His self-esteem is back where it naturally is now, so he has to go have sex with another woman all over again to get his power back up in order for his self-esteem not to feel low. A lot of men wouldn't feel good about themselves if they were virgins, because they would feel like less of a man. They wouldn't fit in with all of their friends. So instead, they go around having sex with women, stealing their energy to make themselves look good. If you are not able to feel good about yourself without having sex with different women, then you need to spend a lot more one on one time with God. You need to allow God to complete you and fill you up to where you don't feel the need to use women to fill yourself up. Take time to yourself, stop having sex, stay in the house, and become one with the creator. Become sucker-free.

Chapter Eight

The G within your Race of People

THE SAYING IS that all people of all races are equal, and all came from God. Although that is true, it doesn't mean being equal didn't come with rules and regulations. *"And whereas thou sawest iron mixed with miry clay, they shall mingle themselves with the seed of men: but they shall not cleave one to another, even as iron is not mixed with clay"- Daniel 2:43 KJV."* Do you all see what Daniel 2:43 is saying? How can you mix and remain united: it is impossible? The iron will only break up the clay from each other. Let's take a look at some evidence. Do you all remember in Genesis when the people tried to build the tower to Heaven to say that they were smarter than God? God saw that as a spit in the face: why would you try to defeat the Creator at his own creations? *"And the lord came down to see the city and the tower, which the children of men builded. And the lord said, behold, the people is one, and they have all one language; and this they begin to do: and nothing will be restrained from them, which they have imagined to do. Go to, let us go down, and there confound their language, that they may not understand one another's speech"- Genesis 11:5-7 KJV.* That is why we have so many languages, types of slang, cultural beliefs, etc.

God is saying I'm going to divide you all, so you all will only have the language I gave you all for your specific race. Now, we can only work with our divine race, since he divided us. All people being on the same page would turn us against him, because we would have too much power. So instead, he turned us against each other. Not made us enemies or anything, but just meant for us to work with our own race of people. *Life is a team sport.* The way God made it is the way he wants it to stay. *"And the sons of Noah, that went forth of the ark were Shem, and Ham, and Japheth: and Ham is the father of Canaan. These are the three sons of Noah: and of them was the whole earth overspread"- Genesis 9:18-19 KJV.* God gave all the races within those nations their own language and territory. Can anyone tell me why God would give every race their own land and language but would still want us to mix?

That is a million-dollar question. You don't see Chinese people having black children. Look at skin texture, hair texture, and body features to exemplify what I am saying. Only the Heavens could produce such a specifically designed human. Now, if God created specifically Blacks, Whites, Mexicans, etc., ask yourself, "Why would He want to mix it?" That would defeat the purpose of creating different races of people. That's like saying even though lions and tigers are animals, it's okay for them to have babies with each other. They both come from the cat family, but we all know, or should know, that lions and tigers are two totally different types of animals. Water and fire don't mix; one eliminates the other. Do you want your race eliminated? I am pretty sure your answer would be no, and if your answer is not no then you are just evil. All I'm saying is stay in your lane when it comes to your race! Let's keep His races pure.

"For God is not the author of confusion, but of peace, as in all churches of the saints"-1 Corinthians 14:33 KJV." God is not a God of confusion; neither is He half a God. Now confusion, for example, could be a child mixed with Black and White, and I am pretty sure that White people and Black people have two different types of family reunions. Correct me if I am wrong, but at Black family reunions there is different music, different dances, different food, and people may be playing dominoes and spades, also. Now, going to those two family reunions just confuses that child. That child doesn't know who they are; it's a whole other world. Now, the half part is saying the child is half White and half Black. Either they're Black or they're White; there is no in between. Either it's a cow or a horse. God doesn't play the in-between game. It's either one or the other; not able to be both. If I were to stay in the house for three years and then come outside, I would still be Black. If I were to move to a Mexican neighborhood, I would still be Black.

No matter how much money you make, where you

live, or the job you have, you are still part of any problem your people are having and part of the solution if you are true to your roots. Nothing, and I do mean nothing will change who you are. You are still labeled as belonging to a particular group of people. There is a reason why job applications, and most of every type of application in the world, ask for your ethnicity. Think about it. My kid is your kid, and your kid is my kid. Your mother is my mother, and vice versa, when you are in the same race. I can prove it with this one question. This question can go for any race on the planet, but it just relates to Blacks more heavily. Why does every Black mother feel threatened, affected, or scared for her Black son when another woman's Black son gets killed by the police, or killed period?

Now, the way the world relates to each other is by money, status, fame, education, neighborhood, etc. God is not a God of favoritism. He doesn't look at that. He divided us into races so we wouldn't look at things like that either. No matter the status or situation, we should always help people of our race. People live by the saying that if you are not on my level, then I am not dealing with you. Money should not separate any race, but it does. We don't even live in the same neighborhood with each other. Every rich person of their race has a responsibility to uplift their people. I'm not talking about buying bikes for Christmas, or turkeys for Thanksgiving, or passing out money. I am talking about schools, businesses, jobs, etc. Things that multiply themselves, things that keep going even when you die.

I love everybody in the world of all races, but I am just following the code. It is a spit in the face to God to go make someone else's race better before you make your own race better. We should be living a sacrificial life for our race. When they hurt, we hurt. When they don't have any money, then we don't have any money. We should go through everything together. No matter if they understand what you are doing, do it anyway. Even if they are not on your level, understand even when you don't understand. Be loyal to God. Better yourself, better your race, and then better everybody else. God comes with instructions. Follow them!

Being a Black man living in America, I understand the value of unity, because we as Black people don't seem to have it, but there is a lot of hope for us. I believe we can and will come together one day. I see the Mexicans, Whites, Asians, Chinese, and other races sticking together. They have their businesses, corporations, neighborhoods, organizations, and etc. Unity within the race is the way to win the race. Look at how birds sick together, or lions, or zebras. They are all one. God is a God of organization, so when he made us the same, he did that so we would know what team we are on. Being Black, Asian, or White is a team you are not able to change, *no matter the circumstance.*

When the LA Lakers lose a game, Kobe also loses. I don't care if Kobe scores fifty points or has the most assists and steals. You play as a team; you lose as a team. There is no "I" in team. When you are on a team, you don't get traded because your team is not doing good at the moment. That is what we do sometimes as a race. We will get our money and degrees and move to a neighborhood of a different race to feel safe, or secure, or like we are more than we are. A lot of people do the things I just named subconsciously, because society has made it normal. I don't care if you are a Black or White person that makes a $1,000,000/year, that shouldn't exempt you from living by a Black or White person of your race that makes $40,000/year or even less. God doesn't show favoritism and neither does he approve of it. Remember, we are doing this for God and not our own personal gain or interest. God says, Love is the greatest commandment. We have to sacrifice for each other no matter the circumstances

Sacrifice

To be a better race, no matter what race you are, you have to sacrifice for the other person. Realize that *it is not all about you*. Your personal wants have to be put on the back burner in order to do what's best for the team. There is a bigger picture other than what we see. We are all little pieces of the puzzle. There is a role that everyone has to play, regardless of the circumstance. If you have ever played basketball, you would know that on defense when the opportunity presents itself, there is someone who has to take the charge (the defensive player allowing the offensive player to run over them with all their force). Usually, a charge is brutal; it hurts. It wasn't for him, but it was for the whole team. I said this saying earlier, *"What you do affects everybody."* It is a chain reaction. If I go to jail, I lose my job, my job loses an employee, and my mother and father lose a son temporarily. They lose money bailing me out of jail. They lose sleep, time, and on and on.

You don't realize the effect you have on a whole cycle by what you do. My friends and I were talking today through group message on our phones. I asked them that if they made a certain amount of money that people in their race don't normally make, would they still stay in the neighborhood where the people of their race don't make the same amount of money? They said they would, but they would do it low-key (where nobody notices). They would live in their bigger house with more money and better job without the community knowing. I understand that they don't want anyone knowing because the things that jealousy can lead to. Jealousy could cause people to rob you, kill you, steal from you, etc. That contradicts the whole sacrificial movement, because if there is something that only you have to offer, then you should offer it. Also, you don't hide things that come from the heart. You should play your position to the fullest. When it is time for you to get in the game, don't shy away from the moment. That is like me being fast in running, and their needing me for a play on the offense for football, but I complain that I don't want to get in the game, because I don't want to get my leg broken, because that would stop me from running fast. There are always going to be consequences. I am just thinking about myself, but my team needs me right now.

"But he that knew not, and did commit things worthy of

stripes, shall be beaten with few stripes. For unto whomsoever much is given, of him shall be much required: and to whom men have committed much, of him they will ask the more"- Luke 12:48 KJV. The more God gives you, the more of the frontline you have to be. He wants to expose your resources and talents, no matter what they are. He isn't concerned about you protecting yourself. He is your protection, he gave you what you have, and only he can take it away. We as people want to protect ourselves, and that is disappointing God. It is like we would rather preserve ourselves, as if we can control what happens to us. *"And when he had called the people unto him with his disciples also, he said unto them, whosoever will come after me, let him deny himself, and take up his cross, and follow me. For whosoever will save his life shall lose it; but whosoever shall lose his life for my sake and the gospel's, the same shall save it"- Mark 8:34-35 KJV.* Choose your realness over your smartness any day. I would rather do what's best for my people than do what's best for myself. When it comes to real sacrifice, you will look *real to God and dumb to the world.*

Unity

To gain all we can gain from unity is to *accept each other for who we are.* Everybody has a role to play, and if we play the role that God has given us, we will continually put the pieces of his puzzle together. We have to understand that every piece of the puzzle is different and may connect to your piece. Do you remember doing civil rights, and things of that nature, around the Martin Luther King Jr.

and Malcolm X era? Malcolm X was for if you hit me, I am going to hit you back, and Martin Luther King Jr. was for peace. See, God is a genius for the way he brought these two people of the same race together at the same time. They were opposite but yet were seeking a common goal, which was to basically help their own race of people. They didn't agree with each other, because they weren't alike, but they put their differences to the side for the enhancement of their race. Martin and Malcolm were each other's strengths; one complemented the other. Or should I say, one picked up where the other left off. To make something work, you have to have two opposites: right or left, up or down, positive or negative, etc. We have to be each other's strengths. It doesn't necessarily matter what you are not good at but what you are good at. Not whether you are lesbian, bisexual, or straight. Not your bad qualities, but your good qualities. How can we use each other to help the overall cause? Football has eleven positions on offense, and basketball has five different positions; I am pretty sure you get the picture. In order to connect *one has to have what the other doesn't.*

Fill the Void

Have you ever looked at a star, the sun, or any other thing that light shines from? You see how they have certain rays, or vibration, that branches out from the center of it. Let's just use the sun as an example. The sun has a lot of rays that branch out from the center of it. Something had to be born from the center of the sun that created that ray to branch out from the sun. Notice I didn't say created, because the rays are already created; the sun just has to give birth to them. It takes all those rays for the sun to be the sun, or for the sun to shine and give heat to the earth. The rays worked together from the power that the sun gave them to make the sun become what it is. Notice that all the rays are coming from different angles. They all have their own distinctive direction or lane, should I say, to add light.

The sun is God, and we, the races, are the rays (don't take that literally, just figuratively). We will only be able to exhibit the light that the sun has to offer if we work together. Every race has the ability to shine and be full of light. Ask yourself, does my race shine, or does my race have the full amount of light that can be exhibited? If your answer is no, then that only means that there is a void that needs to be filled. The only way to fill that void is to play your position. Do what God created you to do. When you fill your void, you have just created a new resource for your race. *Everybody has something that the next person doesn't have.* There may be a lot of empty spaces in our sun, and that is because we don't use what we have to help each other. Your gifts, talents, businesses, ideas, or other endeavors will open a door that the next person needed. When you don't fill that void in your race with your gifts, talents, or resources, you are only blocking everybody from your race. You are keeping a door closed that your fellow neighbor may have needed. You are a thief to your own race. your race won't shine.

What if I am the only person on the block with sugar? Everybody on the block comes to my house to get some sugar, but I don't open the door. First off, not opening the door is relevant to keeping my sun ray from being birthed, keeping my light from shining. Not only will my light not shine, but no one else's light will shine either. Your helping your race is a chain reaction. Everyone in the race is affected.

The sun is God (figuratively). We are just part of the puzzle. The thing is, we have to put them together. The sun doesn't shine from just one, two, or ten rays. It may get a little light, but not enough to be seen. Look at your fellow neighbor, and see how you can fill the void. What strength do you have that covers their weakness? Gifts, talents, resources, or whatever you want to label it. As a race, you are going to have to bring your rays together to create the sun. *Where there is no unity, there is no God.*

Support

To take this a little bit farther, have you ever noticed how the rays on the sun or even a star kind of goes in and out? I believe this is because that is the transfer of energy, or should I say, light. When one fades out, the other ray is brightened. You supported your fellow sun rays, you took the back seat, so they could shine, and they should do the same for you, also. That is the support we need to keep the sun shining in our race. It is like a way we keep our heart beating as a whole race. Without the transfer of energy from one another, the rays will eventually die one by one, and the sun will stop shining, or in other words, our race will die. By people helping each other as a race, it is the transfer of energy from one person to another. We are equally keeping each other alive. It is like a never-ending cycle, kind of like the spinning of the world. We will support your business, and your business will support the church, and the church will support the community to open up new businesses, and the community is the poor, and the poor will work for the businesses. That is a transfer of energy. When one light goes out, another one lights up. That vibration keeps the heart of our race alive. As a race, people should keep that cycle going until the end of time. Do not give off other forms of light to other races. You give to your people, and they give to you.

"Now he that ministereth seed to the sower both minister bread for your food, and multiply your seed sown, and increase the fruits of your righteousness;)"- 2 Corinthians 9:10 KJV. It is just like marketing: you get more out of what you put in, and so on, and so on. Look at it like this, when you are giving to someone of your race, you are giving to God. I am a Black man, and a Black man is me. When I look in the mirror, I see every Black man that ever existed, and every Black man should see me. I live for my race, and my race lives for me. That is the same for your race, and when you *give to other races other than your race, you are stealing from yourself; you are stealing from God.*

Elevation or Elimination

It takes a team to find blessings. If we have two different outlooks based on what we have been through, then we want to feel one another. In other words, we won't have a spiritual connection to one another. How can you understand me if you haven't been through what I've been through? We are who we are: don't live a lie. *"Iron sharpeneth iron; so a man sharpeneth the countenance of his friend"- Proverbs 27:17 KJV.* Now, the verse clearly says that "iron sharpens iron." It doesn't say iron sharpens plastic, or anything other than what it is. Plastic is not able to help iron, and iron is not able to help plastic. Either you elevate or get eliminated. A lot of people would say that that verse stands for intelligent people making intelligent people more intelligent because they see things on an equivalent level, but I personally believe you can use this verse in different directions. With that being said, I believe it's safe to say that on another level, Blacks sharpen blacks, Whites sharpen Whites, and Hispanics sharpen Hispanics, because they see the things on the same level, or at least they should, because before you are smart, intelligent, or anything, you were a Black, White, Hispanic, Japanese, or other race of man or woman. God has his hand on every race, but we have to stay in your own lane and worry about your own people first. Do you make sure your house is clean before you walk out the door? If you answered yes, then you should understand what I'm saying.

My mother said something one day that stuck with me. She said, "What if every Black man from this day forward has sex with a woman of another race, eventually the other race would die off." In biblical text *"Ye are the children of the prophets, and of the covenant which God made with our fathers, saying unto Abraham, and in thy seed shall all the kindreds of the earth be blessed"- Acts 3:25 KJV.* The man holds the race in his genitals. He is the seed planter; he has the power to produce what he wants to produce. Therefore, Black people would still exist if Black men did what my mother said. So let's switch the roles right quick to interpret her statement in a different way. Let's say all Black women stopped having sex with Black men and became impregnated by men of other races. Now, the men of the other races control what is being produced; they are now the seed planters. What if the children born from that seed are taught by their father to have babies with people of his race? Slowly but surely, Black people will be eliminated off the face of the earth. Now, that can be true for any race. You have just eliminated the God-given hair texture, color of skin, shape of lips, shape of ears, culture, history, and etc. To God, that is abomination, the same as abortion. You aborted God's creation. You eliminated what God's was about to create. You are in a form of abomination every time you put your seed into another race's garden, and I am not just talking about sex. That seed could be your time, your resources, your money, your labor, your culture, your talents, etc. That race can take whatever you gave them and just give it to their race.

Don't put your power in the hand of another individual. That is a broad quote, but I am referring to the image of races. They giving the power you gave them to their race is only elevating their race and eliminating your race. Subconsciously, we as races are in competition with one another. See, naturally God created the world for races to have their own lanes, to do their own thing. That is one of the distinctive creations of God. He knew we would be in competition if we realized the differences we have from one another, but it wasn't his intentions.

So, for a race to use what you give them for their own race is only their natural instinct, or should be. The more they get from you, the less you have. For the world to be at peace from a racial perspective, each race has to do their own thing. They have to build within each other and only plant seeds within their race. Don't build someone else a house, and not build yourself one. As a human, would you have the right to be mad if when you finish building another race a house, and they decide not to let you in? Now you are on the outside looking dumb. Everything I said earlier in this chapter will play a part in whether your race gets elevated or eliminated.

CHAPTER NINE
UNLOCK THE CHURCH WITHIN YOU

YOUR CHURCH IS where your heart is. "What do you mean—I thought church was somewhere we go?" I know you probably have been told that a church is only in a building on Sundays. Church is when two or more unite in the name of God. For example, your church can be a football field, when on the football field is where there is brotherhood, unity, love, support, sacrifice, etc. You all are one; everything you do is for the team. You would die on the football field if you had to.

Your church is where you do the most teaching. The center of your soul. The part of you that has the most God in it. Where most of your passion comes from. If people were to see your purpose, or where your heart is, and how you present yourself on a day-to-day basis, would they be able to compare the two? Do you look and act the same way on the outside as you do on the inside, and vice versa?

There is a world inside of you that you should bring to light, where everything about you says what you do as a purpose. Say for instance you see a fashion designer; you will expect to see them in some fashionable clothes with a lot of creativity on a day-to-day basis. That fashion designer defines their purpose without people actually knowing what they do. When your purpose connects to your everyday life, there is no way you can lose. Your spirit connecting to your God- Given purpose is advertising for God. You are showing the world about the God in you and why they should buy into what you have to offer. It should be written all on you through actions, personality, etc. If you haven't already, one day you will wake up and get tired of faking the real you.

Your body and soul should be twins. When people look in the clothing store, music store, bookstore, television screen, hospital, stage, church house, business, college degree of your choice, football/basketball/track field, beauty/barbershop, or any other purpose there might be, they should ask, "Do the product and the person look alike? Do you look like what you are selling? Or are you false advertising, selling or doing something that you wouldn't buy or do yourself?"

Be the Shepherd of Your Church

Like Jesus says in the bible in *John 10:11 KJV,* *"I am the good shepherd: the good shepherd giveth his life for the sheep."* The shepherd is the person that leads his sheep. A shepherd could be a teacher, and the sheep could be the students.

A shepherd could be a musician, and the sheep could be their fans. A shepherd could be the professional athlete, and the sheep could be the little children that look up to them, or the sheep could be their teammates. A shepherd could be a barber/beautician, and their clients could be the sheep. A shepherd could be a doctor or nurse, and the sheep are their patients. A shepherd could be a pastor, and his congregation could be the sheep. A shepherd could be a father or mother, and the sheep are the children. A shepherd could be a business owner, and the sheep could be their employees and customers. A shepherd could be an author, and his sheep could be the people who read his/her books. A shepherd could be an actor, entertainer, or someone famous, and their sheep could be the people who support or pay to see them. In other words, the shepherd leads, and the sheep follows and supports.

What is the difference between a good shepherd and a bad shepherd? The good shepherd will put their all into what they do. They will walk it, talk it, and live it. They are willing to lay down their life for what they believe in; they are willing to lay down their life for the product they are advertising for God. Whether that be in fashion, politics, sports, religion, beauty, medicine, music, etc. The bad shepherd, on the other hand, will only make it look good. The things they promote will not be equal to the way they live. The bad shepherd is deceiving; they will make you think one thing, and actually be doing something totally different. The bad shepherd makes God look like a liar. The bad shepherd will tell their sheep that they will die for them but is nowhere to be found when it's time to die. The bad shepherd usually is not controlled by themselves. The bad shepherd usually has someone in their pockets. Some are like puppets; they have someone controlling them. Others are just doing it for the money and not the love. Examples of bad shepherd are preachers who will tell you about the word of God from front to back, and tell the truth, but don't live it. They make it sound good; they make it look good, but it's not good. They can only talk about it, but not exhibit it. The same thing goes for the musicians: rappers, R&B singers, gospel singers, rock & roll, etc. The same can go for doctors, lawyers, athletes: no one of any profession is exempt. A lot of times they are controlled by someone that you don't see, or they just don't give a damn about their sheep, and it is all about the profit.

The ones that are controlled by a higher power won't dare get out of line, either, or do something their master doesn't like. When I say get out of line, I mean they won't put their life on the line, job on the line, money in certain places, do certain things, or be around certain people. *To truly market your purpose for god, you have to be willing to die for it.* If you are not willing to die for it, then you shouldn't be doing it.

Invest in Your Church

You know how the top businessmen always speak on how you should make money in your sleep, or let your money work for you. They know how to let money work for them.

They invest in certain things that grow over time, whether a business, stocks, or whatever. Let your spirit make you richer in your sleep, and when I say sleep, I don't mean sleep. I mean let your spirit make you richer spiritually and physically while you are off or not working at your purpose at the moment, like being at the grocery store, or the mall, or just out with the family, on a date, or doing anything that can be seen publicly. Instead of investing money in businesses like the businessman, you invest your money in clothes that define you, hobbies that define you, conversations that define you, character that defines you, style that defines you, etc. Even though those things cost money, they will help your arena grow for you. You paid $100 or $200 to get your hair and nails done. That is just an estimate. Not only are you doing this for you, but for everybody supporting you. Your arena or purpose is not only for you. You are representing the cultural aspect of you and everybody who supports you. How can you be a beautician, and your hair not be done? In the long run, you will make all that money back tenfold if you represent your arena or purpose in the correct way. People see you, and they see your church all in one. You could just be out and about, but if your church doesn't align up with what you offer, then you are out of alignment with your spirit.

I know you have seen when a famous person starts wearing a specific brand of clothing, not because someone told them to, but because that is just what they like. Then all of a sudden, the clothing brand starts paying them to wear their clothing. That is the same way with God. When you let your spirit guide you to do what God feels is best for you in every area of your life outside your church, then He will too start paying you for supporting His brand. You can be at the grocery store on your off day representing for your church, and that could bring you more customers, fans, patients, etc., just by how you let your spirit guide you. Let's say you are a personal trainer, and you are at the grocery store shopping for food. You just so happen to have on some gym clothes. A potential client, or let's say someone that really wants to get in shape but doesn't have the motivation, sees you. You are putting healthy food items in your basket for the most part and look like you just came from the gym. You all may pass each other and spark a conversation, and the way you live outside the gym will motivate the potential client to take getting in shape more seriously. Even if you didn't even start a conversation, or if they didn't even know what you did for a living, just the way they seen you outside your church will inspire them. Get inside the spiritual Maybach God has for you, and let Him be your chauffeur, and watch how much richer you become in every area without lifting a single finger. *"And we know that all things work together for good to them that love God, to them who are called according to his purpose"- Romans 8:28 KJV.* Allow everything in your day-to-day life to add up and equal your purpose. I am referring to your conversations, to the clothes you wear, to your character, to your personality, to your habits, and all other things. *You are the best brand that you could ever represent.*

Pave the Way for Your Teammates

You know how in John 13 when Jesus washed his disciples' feet, *"If I then, your lord and master, have washed your feet; ye also ought to wash one another's feet. For I have given you an example, that ye should do as I have done to you"- John 13:14-15 KJV.* Even though he was the leader, he was showing how one should be humble enough to serve one another no matter the position. Jesus was setting an example to His fellow disciples, or teammates, as I would say. He couldn't accept them if they weren't willing to be humiliated for each other. I know you have heard the saying, "A chain is only as strong as its weakest link." When paving the way, be the first to step outside the box; take the risk. The way can only be paved when someone opens the lane for others to walk down. *You have to embarrass yourself in order for your teammates to look good.* In this case, your teammates are a part of your arena. Hip-hop pioneers have paved the way for hip-hop artists. The first Black quarterback in the NFL paved the way for other black quarterbacks. Do not wait for someone else to take the first step in brooding your church. There is something that everybody is thinking, but nobody wants to be the first to do it. Someone has to make themselves look bad, so the rest of the team can look good. When dealing with God, He may tell you to do some embarrassing things to show your loyalty toward your church that He placed you in. Little do you know, the door you are opening is for everybody that comes behind you. Jesus knew that dying on the cross would allow people to live through Him, but if he had never listened to God, he would've kept that door closed and blocked people from being able to live through Him. Like something just as James Brown saying, "I'm Black and I'm proud!" He made Black people proud of who they were. He embarrassed himself for them. Believe me, somebody wanted to say it but just didn't. He paved the way for happiness of being Black. You can think of Bill Gates dropping out of college to create Microsoft. The fact that he created Microsoft was not the point. He and others paved the way for other internet geniuses. It is a long line of people who were called dumb and ignorant for being the first ones to take chances that no one else would take.

"So the last shall be first, and the first last: for many be called, but few chosen"—Matthew 20:16 KJV. The ones that everyone doubted and looked down upon will be the same ones that everyone looks up to. Be one of the ones who is looked up to. When you do that, you will win not only for yourself, but for everybody. Whatever it is that you love, or whatever church of life God has placed you in, He has placed you to pave the way for people who are going to come behind you. *Who will be the first to do it; if you don't do it first?* Your light will show others the light. Your idea will spark other people's ideas.

The Message

I KNOW THAT we as people go through life drifting back and forth, up and down, left and right, through good and evil, not really having an equilibrium. We go through life trying to find the balance between being a perfect imperfection, knowing that we are not able to be perfect, but still striving to be the perfect us.

We tend to fall into all types of traps that the world has set before us without having a specific code that we live by. We say God's word is the same today and forever, but we don't exhibit it in our day to-day lives. God will continue to be God, and the Devil will continue to be the Devil. The Devil finds new traps and different ways to trick us out of our position from generation to generation. The Devil will always trick us into judging someone, the Devil will always trick you into spending money, the Devil will always trick you into not being yourself, the Devil will always trick you into thinking with your dick one way or the other, the Devil will always trick you into believing that church is just a building you go to on Sundays when in reality the church is within you, the church is your purpose, and the more we get tricked out of our position the more we leave God's Code behind.

The code is there to give you stability to operate in life, to help you become more of one with the creator. See, God stays the same, but the Devil changes. God's Code will defeat any change that the Devil makes. The code will unlock a person in you that is at peace, knowing that you will be the same tomorrow, next month, and next year, because God's Word will never come back void. Once God unlocks you, you become limitless.

When you follow the world, and not a specific set of rules, you will forever change. Your emotions will forever control your actions, and emotions will be different everyday as long as there is a world to live on. Know that the rules you follow today will work ten years from now, or even an hundred years from now even though millions of things have changed. *You obey the code, and the world will forever follow you; you don't obey the code and you will forever follow the world.*

Author's Social Media Accounts

Instagram: wise_by_nature
Facebook: Demetrice DeeDee Chance
Periscope: Wise_by_Nature

Made in the USA
Columbia, SC
15 September 2019